WHAT TO KNOW BEFORE YOU GO

A Tourist's Guide to Iceland

Expert Advice on When to Visit, How to Get
There and Around, Where to Stay, What to
Do, Local Customs, and more.

Ronald N. Chambers

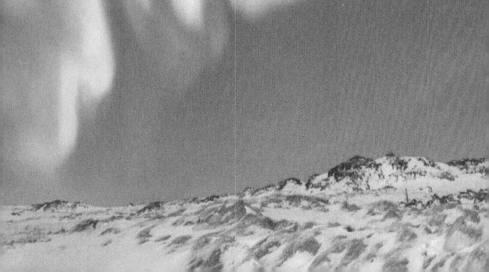

TABLE OF CONTENTS

INTRODUCTION

Iceland is a land that captures the imagination with its breathtaking landscapes, unique culture, and intriguing history. Known for its rugged terrain and natural wonders, this island offers something for every traveler, from adventure seekers to those who simply want to relax and soak in its beauty. However, while Iceland's attractions are well-known, preparing for a trip to this one-of-a-kind destination requires more than just picking a few spots on the map. It's essential to understand the practicalities of traveling here, as this will make your trip much smoother and allow you to fully enjoy what this extraordinary country has to offer.

This guide is designed to provide a clear, straightforward look at everything you need to know before stepping foot in Iceland. Whether you're planning to chase the Northern Lights, look around the glaciers, or experience the vibrant culture of Reykjavik, being prepared is key. This book covers the essential details to make your trip to Iceland both enjoyable and stress-free. Many travelers are surprised to learn that things like packing, transportation, and even the local currency can be quite different from what they're used to. Iceland's weather is unpredictable, and if you're not prepared, it can quickly catch you off guard. Knowing what to bring and how to move around efficiently will save you time and prevent unnecessary headaches.

For those wondering how to get to Iceland, this guide provides clear options, whether you're flying directly from major cities or exploring alternative routes. And once you arrive, navigating the country becomes an adventure of its own. Iceland's public transport may be limited in some areas, and getting around often involves renting a car or relying on local transportation apps. Each option comes with its own pros and cons, and this guide gives you a complete understanding of what will work best for your trip.

Money matters are another important aspect to consider before you arrive. Iceland is known for being a bit pricey, but with the right planning, you can enjoy everything it offers without breaking the bank. Currency exchange, local prices, and tips for managing your budget are all outlined in a way that's easy to follow. On top of that, knowing the basics of Icelandic electricity, plug adapters, and internet connectivity will ensure you're fully equipped for your stay.

Of course, every country has its own set of local customs and laws, and Iceland is no exception. Learning about these in advance will not only help you fit in better with the locals but also keep you from making any embarrassing or disrespectful mistakes. Simple things, like local etiquette and understanding what's considered polite or impolite, can go a long way in making your trip more enjoyable. Even learning a few basic phrases in Icelandic can make a huge difference when interacting with locals, and this guide provides you with key phrases that are easy to remember and useful in everyday situations.

Iceland is also a country that values safety, especially given its sometimes harsh weather conditions. From healthcare services to emergency contacts, it's important to be aware of what to do in case of illness or unexpected events. This guide offers clear instructions on how to access medical care if needed and gives advice on how to stay safe in Iceland's unpredictable weather.

Another important topic covered in this guide is responsible tourism. Iceland's natural beauty is delicate, and many areas are protected for environmental reasons. Respecting these areas not only preserves them for future visitors but also helps maintain the country's ecosystem. By following simple guidelines on how to be a responsible tourist, you'll contribute to keeping Iceland's landscapes as pristine as they've been for centuries.

For travelers who love to immerse themselves in local culture, Iceland offers rich traditions, vibrant festivals, and an exciting arts scene. From local music to art and crafts, there's much to find out. This guide offers suggestions on the best times and places to experience Icelandic culture firsthand, whether through festivals, exhibitions, or simply interacting with local artisans.

When it comes to finding places to stay, Iceland has options for every type of traveler. Whether you're a budget backpacker, a family looking for a cozy cottage, or someone seeking luxury accommodation, this guide breaks down where to stay based on your needs. It even includes tips on finding pet-friendly options or accommodations that cater to travelers with accessibility needs.

For food lovers, Iceland's cuisine is a highlight in itself. With fresh seafood, traditional dishes, and a growing street food scene, there's plenty to enjoy. This guide will point you to the must-try local dishes and where to find them, whether you're dining at a high-end restaurant or grabbing a bite from a food truck.

Perhaps one of the most exciting parts of visiting Iceland is the variety of outdoor activities and natural attractions. From glacier hikes and geothermal spas to exploring hidden waterfalls and taking scenic drives through the countryside, Iceland offers endless possibilities. But beyond the well-known spots, there are also hidden gems, off-the-beaten-path adventures, and lesser-known sights that many tourists overlook. This guide aims to help you find out those too.

As a final note, it's important to mention that Iceland is a place where careful planning pays off. With its unpredictable weather, unique customs, and many remote areas, being informed ahead of time will ensure your trip goes smoothly. By the time you finish reading this guide, you'll have a strong understanding of what to expect, how to plan, and how to get the most out of your visit to this beautiful and fascinating country.

This book is packed with practical advice, valuable tips, and expert suggestions tailored to help you find your way Iceland with ease. From the moment you begin planning to the time you leave, this guide will serve as your go-to resource, ensuring you have everything you need to make your trip truly memorable.

HOW TO USE THIS GUIDE

Planning a trip can be an exciting yet overwhelming experience, especially when visiting a bustling and dynamic city like Iceland. This guide has been crafted to help you navigate the city with ease, providing you with all the essential information needed to make the most of your visit. Here's how you can make the best use of this guide:

1. Start with the Basics: Before diving into the details, take some time to familiarize yourself with the introductory sections of the book. These sections cover key information about Iceland, including its neighborhoods, local customs, transportation options, and tips for navigating the city efficiently. Understanding these basics will help you feel more confident as you plan your trip.

2. Customize Your Experience: One of the unique aspects of this guide is its flexibility. Instead of offering pre-made itineraries, this book empowers you to create a travel experience that's perfectly tailored to your interests and preferences. Use the information provided in each chapter to decide what attractions, restaurants, and activities appeal most to you.

3. Use the Itinerary Planner: To assist you in organizing your trip, we've included a comprehensive 14-page itinerary planner within the book. This planner is designed to help you document your plans, including daily activities, places to visit, dining options, and more. By filling out the planner as you go through the guide, you'll be able to create a well-structured itinerary that ensures you don't miss out on anything important. Feel free to print out the planner pages, so you can jot down notes and plans as you read.

4. **Explore Each Section at Your Own Pace:** Whether you're interested in famous landmarks, hidden gems, dining experiences, or cultural events, this guide covers a wide range of topics. Take your time exploring each section, and don't feel pressured to rush through. The book is designed to be user-friendly, allowing you to navigate between chapters and topics easily.

5. **Use the Guide On-the-Go:** If you're traveling with a digital version of this book, take advantage of the clickable links and QR codes to access additional resources and maps. This can be especially helpful when you're on the move and need quick access to information.

6. **Revisit Key Sections as Needed:** Depending on the length of your stay and the time of year you visit; you might find yourself revisiting certain sections for updated information or reminders. The guide is structured to be a resource you can return to throughout your trip, ensuring you have the most relevant information at your fingertips.

7. **Adapt the Guide to Your Preferences:** Iceland offers something for every type of traveler, whether you're a solo adventurer, a family on vacation, or a couple seeking romance. Use the chapters focused on specific types of travelers to find recommendations that align with your travel style.

THE HISTORY OF ICELAND

Iceland's history is one of the most fascinating in the world, filled with tales of survival, exploration, and change. Situated in the North Atlantic, this island has been home to settlers, look arounders, and nations seeking to find their place in a harsh but beautiful environment. Understanding Iceland's past offers insight into its culture, its people, and the development of its unique way of life.

The story of Iceland begins around the late 9th century when it was first settled by Norsemen, primarily from Norway. Before this, the island was largely uninhabited, though there are records that suggest monks from Ireland may have visited the land earlier, seeking solitude and religious retreat. These monks, however, did not stay long, and it was the Norse settlers who established permanent roots in Iceland.

The first known settler was Ingólfr Arnarson, a Norwegian chieftain who is believed to have arrived in Iceland around the year 874. He landed in what is now Reykjavík, which later became Iceland's capital city. Over the next few decades, more Norse families followed, primarily fleeing conflicts in Norway or seeking new lands due to limited resources in their homeland. These early settlers faced incredible challenges in adapting to Iceland's rough terrain and extreme climate, but they brought with them knowledge of farming, animal husbandry, and survival that allowed them to establish a foothold on the island.

One of the most important events in Iceland's early history was the formation of the Althing in 930 AD. The Althing is one of the oldest parliamentary institutions in the world and was established as a way to resolve disputes among the settlers. Without a king or central authority, Iceland operated under a system of chieftains, each controlling their own areas. The Althing provided a place where these chieftains could meet to discuss laws, resolve conflicts, and make decisions for the wider community. Held annually at Thingvellir, a location not far from Reykjavík, the Althing was not only a gathering for legal matters but also a social event, where people from across the island could meet, trade, and share news.

During the 10th and 11th centuries, Iceland's settlers converted from their traditional Norse pagan beliefs to Christianity. This transition was relatively peaceful compared to other parts of Europe, where religious conversions were often forced or accompanied by violence. In Iceland, the decision to adopt Christianity was made at the Althing in the year 1000. The shift was a pragmatic one, as Icelandic leaders sought to avoid the divisions that religious differences could cause. The transition allowed pagan practices to continue in private for some time, while public life gradually shifted to Christian customs.

The medieval period in Iceland was marked by the growth of farming communities, with sheep farming and fishing becoming the primary means of sustenance. Due to the island's isolation, Iceland developed a distinct culture, with strong oral traditions that passed down stories, histories, and laws. One of the most famous examples of this oral tradition is the Icelandic sagas. These sagas, written down in the 13th century but based on earlier oral stories, are a collection of historical narratives that tell the tales of Icelandic families, heroes, and events. The sagas are an invaluable source for understanding Iceland's early history, culture, and values, and they remain a significant part of Icelandic identity today.

By the 13th century, Iceland had entered into a period known as the Age of the Sturlungs, named after one of the most powerful families of the time. This period was marked by intense conflicts between rival chieftains, leading to a civil war that weakened the island's social and political structure. These internal conflicts made Iceland vulnerable to external influences, and in 1262, Iceland came under the rule of the Norwegian crown. This agreement, known as the Old Covenant, marked the end of Iceland's independence for several centuries. Although Iceland retained its local government institutions, such as the Althing, it was now subject to the authority of the Norwegian king.

In the late 14th century, Norway entered into a union with Denmark, and as a result, Iceland came under Danish rule. For the next several centuries, Iceland's fortunes were tied to those of Denmark. The island became increasingly isolated, with limited contact with the rest of Europe. Trade was tightly controlled by Denmark, and Iceland's economy remained primarily agricultural, with limited development in other areas. This period was difficult for Icelanders, as the harsh climate and frequent volcanic eruptions made survival challenging. The eruption of the Laki volcano in 1783 was particularly devastating, leading to widespread famine and death, as much of the island's livestock was lost.

The 19th century brought significant changes to Iceland. Across Europe, nationalist movements were growing, and Icelanders began to seek more control over their own affairs. Denmark's grip on Iceland weakened, and a movement for independence gained momentum. In 1845, the Althing, which had been suspended for a time, was re-established as a consultative assembly. Iceland's leaders began pushing for greater autonomy, and by 1874, Denmark granted Iceland its own constitution, allowing for limited self-governance. This was an important step toward independence, but it would take several more decades for Iceland to fully break free from Danish rule.

Iceland's path to full independence was solidified during the early 20th century. In 1918, Iceland became a sovereign state under the Danish crown, with its own flag and foreign policy, though Denmark still controlled some aspects of Iceland's government. However, the outbreak of World War II had a significant impact on Iceland's relationship with Denmark. Denmark was occupied by Germany in 1940, cutting off communication between the two countries. Iceland, meanwhile, was occupied by British and later American forces, as its strategic location in the North Atlantic was crucial to the Allied war effort.

After the war, Iceland seized the opportunity to declare full independence. On June 17, 1944, while Denmark was still recovering from the war, Iceland officially became a republic.

A new constitution was adopted, and the Althing, which had existed in various forms for over a thousand years, became the nation's fully sovereign parliament. The first president of Iceland, Sveinn Björnsson, was elected on this same day.

In the years following independence, Iceland underwent significant modernization. The economy, once dominated by farming and fishing, began to diversify, though fishing remained a central part of the nation's livelihood. The mid-20th century saw Iceland enter into several important agreements that shaped its modern identity, including joining NATO in 1949. The country also engaged in the so-called "Cod Wars" with Britain, a series of disputes over fishing rights in the North Atlantic. These conflicts highlighted the importance of fishing to Iceland's economy and its determination to protect its resources.

Today, Iceland is known for its thriving tourism industry, which has grown rapidly in recent years thanks to the island's stunning natural beauty, including its glaciers, volcanoes, and waterfalls. However, Iceland has also made strides in other areas, including renewable energy, as it is a global leader in harnessing geothermal and hydroelectric power. While the country's history is deeply rooted in its early settlers and harsh survival conditions, it has transformed into a modern, forward-thinking nation that continues to attract people from all over the world.

The history of Iceland is a story of resilience, adaptability, and a people who have managed to thrive in one of the most challenging environments on Earth. From its early Norse settlers to its emergence as an independent republic, Iceland's past is a key to understanding its present. Each chapter in the island's history has contributed to its unique culture, and its ability to maintain traditions while embracing change makes Iceland one of the most interesting nations to look around today.

WHY YOU SHOULD VISIT ICELAND

Iceland is one of the most remarkable places you can visit as a tourist, offering experiences that are hard to find anywhere else in the world. From its natural beauty to its rich culture, there are countless reasons why Iceland should be on your list of must-visit destinations. The island is often described as otherworldly because of its incredible landscapes that are unlike anything you'll see elsewhere.

One of the most compelling reasons to visit Iceland is its extraordinary scenery. The country is home to a wide variety of natural wonders, from massive glaciers and powerful waterfalls to volcanic landscapes and hot springs. One of the most famous attractions is the Blue Lagoon, a geothermal spa that is set in a lava field. The warm, mineral-rich waters of the lagoon provide a relaxing experience that many visitors consider a highlight of their trip. But the Blue Lagoon is just one example of the geothermal activity that defines Iceland. There are countless hot springs across the country where you can bathe and relax, often with a beautiful backdrop of mountains or rugged terrain.

Another reason to visit Iceland is its incredible waterfalls. Some of the most famous include Gullfoss, Skógafoss, and Seljalandsfoss. These waterfalls are not only visually stunning but also easily accessible, allowing you to get up close and feel the power of the water. For many tourists, these waterfalls are a major draw, and each one offers a different experience, whether it's walking behind the cascading water of Seljalandsfoss or feeling the sheer force of Gullfoss as it plunges into a deep canyon.

In addition to its waterfalls, Iceland is famous for its glaciers. These massive sheets of ice cover roughly 11% of the country and offer visitors the chance to hike, look around ice caves, or even snowmobile across their frozen surfaces. Vatnajökull, the largest glacier in Europe, is located in Iceland, and within it lies an extraordinary sight: the crystal-clear ice caves. These natural formations are a seasonal attraction that draws tourists from around the world, offering a glimpse into the frozen beauty of the country's glaciers.

For those who enjoy outdoor adventures, Iceland offers many activities, including hiking, bird watching, and whale watching. The country is crisscrossed with well-marked hiking trails that cater to both beginners and experienced hikers. The Laugavegur Trail, for instance, is one of the most famous multi-day hikes in the world, taking hikers through an incredible variety of landscapes, including colorful mountains, hot springs, and volcanic deserts. Bird watching is also popular, with puffins being one of the main attractions during the summer months. Iceland's coastal waters are rich in marine life, and going on a whale-watching tour is a great way to see these magnificent creatures up close.

Another reason to visit Iceland is the opportunity to witness the Northern Lights, also known as the Aurora Borealis. This natural light display, caused by solar particles interacting with the Earth's magnetic field, is a breathtaking sight that draws people from all over the world. The best time to see the

Northern Lights is during the winter months when the skies are darkest, and many travelers specifically plan their trips around this incredible natural phenomenon. Iceland's remote location and clear skies make it one of the best places in the world to view the Northern Lights.

If you are interested in history and culture, Iceland has plenty to offer as well. The country's history dates back to the Viking Age, and you can learn about this era by visiting the National Museum of Iceland or exploring sites such as Þingvellir, the location of Iceland's ancient parliament, the Althing. Þingvellir is not only historically significant but also a place of great natural beauty, with rift valleys formed by the tectonic plates that lie beneath the island. Icelandic culture is deeply connected to its past, and throughout the country, you'll find museums and landmarks that tell the story of its early settlers, its struggles, and its achievements.

One of the best things about visiting Iceland is the opportunity to experience its unique culture. The Icelandic people are known for their friendliness and hospitality, and they take great pride in their traditions. Whether you're enjoying a traditional Icelandic meal, listening to local music, or participating in one of the many festivals held throughout the year, you'll get a sense of the strong cultural identity that defines this nation. Icelandic cuisine is also something to look around, with dishes that feature fresh seafood, lamb, and dairy products. For a truly local experience, try dishes like hákarl (fermented shark), skyr (a type of yogurt), and lamb soup, which has been a staple of Icelandic cooking for centuries.

Iceland is also a great destination for those looking for a peaceful retreat. Despite the growing popularity of the country as a tourist destination, there are still many places where you can find solitude and quiet. The rural landscapes, small villages, and remote locations provide an ideal setting for relaxation and reflection. Whether you're soaking in a hot spring surrounded by snow-covered mountains or walking along a black sand beach with nothing but the sound of the waves, Iceland offers an escape from the busyness of everyday life.

For photographers, Iceland is a dream destination. The dramatic landscapes, changing light conditions, and natural phenomena such as geysers, waterfalls, and ice caves provide endless opportunities for capturing stunning images. Even if you're not a professional photographer, you'll find yourself taking more pictures than you ever thought possible, as the beauty of Iceland demands to be captured.

Another advantage of visiting Iceland is the country's commitment to sustainability and responsible tourism. Icelanders have a deep respect for their natural environment, and this is reflected in the way the country manages its tourism industry. From protecting fragile ecosystems to promoting renewable energy (Iceland is powered almost entirely by geothermal and hydroelectric energy), the country has set a positive example for how tourism and conservation can coexist. Visitors are encouraged to follow guidelines that help preserve the beauty of the landscape, such as staying on marked paths and avoiding littering.

Iceland is also known for its accessibility. Even though it is a small island nation, it is easy to get to, with frequent flights from major cities in Europe and North America. Once in Iceland, the road system is well-developed, and many of the country's most famous sights are located along the Ring Road, a highway that circles the island. This makes it easy for tourists to look around the country, whether they're renting a car or joining a guided tour. Additionally, Iceland's capital city, Reykjavík, is a charming and vibrant place to spend time. With its colorful houses, lively arts scene, and excellent restaurants, it provides a perfect contrast to the wild landscapes found elsewhere on the island.

For those interested in learning more about the world's geological history, Iceland is an open book. The island sits on top of the Mid-Atlantic Ridge, a boundary between the North American and Eurasian tectonic plates. This unique location means that Iceland experiences regular volcanic activity, which has shaped the country's landscapes over millions of years. Visitors can witness this geological activity firsthand by visiting volcanoes, lava fields, and geothermal areas. Iceland is one of the few places in the world where you can see the effects of two tectonic plates pulling apart, and this geological uniqueness adds to the country's appeal.

There are countless reasons why Iceland is a destination that should not be missed. The country's incredible natural beauty, rich cultural history, and opportunities for adventure make it an ideal location for any traveler. Whether you're looking to look around glaciers, witness the Northern Lights, soak in hot springs, or simply experience a place unlike any other, Iceland has it all. It's a place where you can connect with nature, learn about a unique culture, and create memories that will last a lifetime. With its friendly people, stunning landscapes, and endless activities, Iceland offers an experience that is truly unforgettable.

CHAPTER 1

PREPARING FOR YOUR TRIP TO ICELAND

Visa and Entry Requirements

If you are planning to visit Iceland as a tourist, understanding the visa and entry requirements is crucial for a smooth trip. The specific requirements for entry depend on your nationality, the purpose of your visit, and the length of your stay. Iceland is part of the Schengen Area, which consists of several European countries that have agreed to allow free movement across their borders. This means that the visa policies of Iceland are closely aligned with those of other Schengen countries, but there are still certain guidelines and procedures that need to be followed depending on your situation.

For citizens of countries that are part of the Schengen Area, such as most of Europe, visiting Iceland is relatively simple. If you are a national of one of these countries, you can travel to Iceland without the need for a visa. You are allowed to stay for up to 90 days within a 180-day period for tourism or business purposes. This means that if you spend 90 days in any Schengen country (including Iceland), you must wait another 90 days before returning, unless you have a residence permit or a long-term visa. However, even though you do not need a visa, it's important to carry a valid passport or national ID card, as you may be asked to present it upon entry.

For those traveling from outside the Schengen Area, the visa requirements depend on the agreements between Iceland and your home country. Citizens of several non-Schengen countries, including the United States, Canada, Australia, New Zealand, Japan, and South Korea, can also visit Iceland without a visa for up to 90 days within a 180-day period. However, they must still comply with the Schengen rules regarding the length of stay and may be required to provide proof of return or onward travel, sufficient funds, and valid travel insurance when entering Iceland. Even though a visa is not required for short stays, you should ensure your passport is valid for at least three months beyond your intended departure date from the Schengen Area.

For tourists from countries that are not exempt from visa requirements, you will need to apply for a Schengen visa before traveling to Iceland. This type of visa allows you to enter Iceland and other Schengen countries for up to 90 days within a 180-day period. The application process for a Schengen visa involves submitting a range of documents to the Icelandic consulate or embassy in your country. These documents typically include a completed visa application form, a valid passport, recent passport-sized photos, proof of travel insurance, flight reservations, accommodation bookings, and proof of financial means to cover your stay in Iceland. You may also be required to provide a cover letter explaining the purpose of your visit and a detailed travel itinerary. Processing times for Schengen visas can vary, so it's recommended to apply well in advance of your planned departure to allow time for any delays.

When applying for a Schengen visa to visit Iceland, there are a few important details to keep in mind. First, the visa application process requires you to submit biometric data, including fingerprints and a digital photograph, unless you have provided this data within the past five years. The visa fee is generally non-refundable, even if your application is rejected. Additionally, approval of a Schengen visa does not automatically guarantee entry into Iceland. Border officials at the airport or other entry points have the right to ask for additional documentation, such as proof of accommodation, a return ticket, or sufficient funds, and can deny entry if they believe you do not meet the entry requirements or pose a risk to security.

If you plan to stay in Iceland for longer than 90 days or are visiting for reasons other than tourism (such as work, study, or joining family members), you will need to apply for a long-term visa or residence permit. Long-term visas for Iceland are not covered under the Schengen visa framework, so the process and requirements are different. Depending on your situation, you may need to provide additional documentation, such as a work contract, proof of enrollment in an educational institution, or marriage certificates if you are joining a spouse. Applications for long-term stays must be submitted directly to the Directorate of Immigration in Iceland or through the appropriate embassy or consulate in your home country.

Regardless of whether you need a visa to enter Iceland, there are certain standard entry requirements that apply to all visitors. Upon arrival in Iceland, immigration officials may ask you to provide documents such as your passport, return flight details, proof of accommodation, and travel insurance. Iceland requires all visitors to have travel insurance that covers medical expenses and emergency medical evacuation for the duration of their stay. The insurance must be valid throughout the Schengen Area, and it is advisable to carry proof of coverage with you. In addition, it is important to have enough financial means to support yourself during your stay in Iceland. This can include access to credit cards, cash, or other forms of proof that you have the financial resources to cover accommodation, meals, and other expenses while traveling in the country.

For travelers who have a criminal record or have been previously denied entry to Iceland or any other Schengen country, entry into Iceland may be more complicated. In some cases, you may be required to provide additional documentation or may even be refused entry depending on the severity of your past infractions. It's always advisable to check with the Icelandic authorities or an immigration lawyer if you are unsure about your eligibility to enter the country.

It is also important to note that Iceland is not part of the European Union, but it is part of the European Economic Area (EEA), which means it follows many of the same regulations when it comes to the movement of people and goods. However, if you are an EU or EEA citizen, you have the right to live and work in Iceland without a visa or residence permit, though you will need to register with the local authorities if you plan to stay for more than three months.

Lastly, Iceland has strict regulations when it comes to bringing goods into the country. While Iceland does not impose duties on personal belongings, there are limits on the amount of alcohol, tobacco, and certain food items that can be brought into the country. Iceland also has restrictions on bringing in plants, animals, and certain medications. If you are carrying prescription drugs, it's advisable to bring a doctor's note or prescription to avoid any issues at customs. It's always best to declare any items that may be restricted to avoid fines or confiscation of goods.

The Best Time to Visit

The best time to visit Iceland depends heavily on what you want to experience during your trip. Iceland is known for its diverse and sometimes extreme weather, which changes dramatically with the seasons. The country offers a variety of experiences throughout the year, and understanding the differences between each season will help you decide when to plan your visit.

Many tourists choose to visit Iceland during the summer months, which typically span from June to August. Summer is the most popular time for travelers, and there are several reasons for this. First, the weather is at its warmest during this time of year. While Iceland's summer temperatures are mild by global standards, typically ranging between 10°C to 15°C (50°F to 59°F), they are still far more pleasant for outdoor exploration than the cold winter months. The longer days during summer are another major draw. From mid-May to late July, Iceland experiences the phenomenon of the Midnight Sun, where daylight stretches for nearly 24 hours. In some places, especially in the northern parts of the country, the sun barely dips below the horizon, making it possible to look around the outdoors late into the night. For travelers who want to make the most of their time exploring Iceland's natural beauty, the extended daylight offers the opportunity to pack more activities into each day.

Summer also offers the best conditions for hiking and exploring some of Iceland's more remote areas. Roads leading to highland regions, like the famous Laugavegur trail, are often impassable during the winter due to snow. But in summer, the roads are open, and the trails are more accessible, making it the ideal time to look around Iceland's highlands, which are filled with stunning landscapes of volcanic deserts, glacial rivers, and geothermal springs. Furthermore, summer is the perfect time for those who wish to visit Iceland's famous waterfalls, like Gullfoss and Seljalandsfoss, as the snowmelt from the mountains adds volume to the waterfalls, making them even more impressive.

Another summer highlight is the chance to observe Iceland's rich wildlife. Birdwatchers, in particular, flock to the country to see puffins, which nest on Iceland's cliffs from May to August. Additionally, whale watching tours are most successful during the summer, as whales migrate to Iceland's waters to feed. Tourists can often spot humpback whales, minke whales, and even orcas on these tours.

However, the summer months are also the busiest in terms of tourist numbers. Popular attractions like the Blue Lagoon, the Golden Circle, and Reykjavík can become crowded with visitors. If you prefer quieter, less crowded destinations, this is something to keep in mind when planning your trip.

If you're looking to avoid the summer crowds but still want relatively mild weather, the shoulder seasons – spring (April to May) and autumn (September to October) – can be ideal times to visit Iceland. During these months, the weather is cooler than summer but warmer than winter, with temperatures ranging from 0°C to 10°C (32°F to 50°F). While daylight is not as long as during the summer, you still get a decent amount of daylight for sightseeing. In spring, you can witness the landscape as it begins to thaw, with blooming flowers and green fields making the scenery even more beautiful. In autumn, the changing colors of the leaves add a new dimension to Iceland's landscapes, particularly around the countryside.

Spring and autumn also offer a chance to enjoy some of Iceland's most popular attractions without the summer crowds. You'll find fewer tourists at major sights like the Golden Circle and the South Coast, giving you a more peaceful experience. Prices for accommodations and tours also tend to be lower during these months compared to the peak summer season, making it a good option for budget-conscious travelers.

For those who dream of seeing the Northern Lights, winter is the best time to visit Iceland. From late September to mid-April, the long nights provide the perfect conditions for viewing this natural phenomenon. The Northern Lights, or

Aurora Borealis, are caused by solar particles interacting with the Earth's magnetic field, and they create stunning displays of green, pink, and purple lights dancing across the sky. Many tourists visit Iceland specifically to see the Northern Lights, and although they are never guaranteed, the best chance of witnessing them is during the dark winter months.

However, winter in Iceland brings challenges that travelers should be prepared for. Temperatures can drop significantly, ranging from -1°C to 5°C (30°F to 41°F), and strong winds and snowstorms are not uncommon. Additionally, daylight is limited, especially in December and January, when the sun only rises for a few hours each day. Despite the cold, many tourists still visit during the winter months to experience the beauty of Iceland under a blanket of snow. The frozen waterfalls, snow-covered mountains, and icy glaciers create a magical atmosphere that is quite different from the summer landscape.

Winter also offers unique activities that are not available during other seasons. For example, ice cave tours are a popular winter attraction. These caves, formed within glaciers, are only accessible during the colder months when the ice is stable enough to enter. The inside of these caves glows with a surreal blue light, making them one of the most stunning natural wonders Iceland has to offer. Additionally, winter is a great time to relax in one of Iceland's many geothermal hot springs, which are even more inviting when the air is cold and crisp.

For those who don't mind the cold and want to experience Iceland in a quieter, more peaceful setting, winter can be a rewarding time to visit. However, it's important to be aware of the potential for difficult travel conditions. Snow and ice can make some roads impassable, particularly in remote areas, and it's essential to check weather conditions and road closures before heading out. Renting a car with four-wheel drive is recommended if you plan on driving during the winter, and many visitors opt to join guided tours instead to avoid the challenges of winter driving.

In addition to the natural wonders that change with the seasons, Iceland also hosts a variety of festivals and cultural events throughout the year. For example, the Reykjavík Arts Festival, held in May, showcases local and international artists through exhibitions, performances, and concerts. In August, the city also hosts the Reykjavík Pride Festival, which celebrates Iceland's inclusive and welcoming LGBTQ+ community. Winter brings its own set of festivities, including the Winter Lights Festival in February, which features light installations and cultural events throughout Reykjavík.

The best time to visit Iceland depends on what you want to experience. If you prefer mild weather, long days, and outdoor adventures, summer is the ideal time to visit. For those interested in seeing the Northern Lights or experiencing the country's winter beauty, the colder months are best. And if you want to avoid the crowds while still enjoying relatively good weather, the shoulder seasons of spring and autumn provide a good balance. No matter when you visit, Iceland's natural beauty and unique experiences make it a destination worth exploring year-round.

PACKING ESSENTIALS FOR VISITING ICELAND

When preparing for a trip to Iceland, packing the right essentials is key to ensuring that you are comfortable and well-prepared for whatever the weather and landscape may throw at you. Iceland's climate can be unpredictable, and the landscape is both beautiful and rugged, which means your packing list will need to cover a wide range of possibilities.

One of the most important things to keep in mind when packing for Iceland is the weather. Iceland's climate can change rapidly, sometimes even within the same day. It is common to experience sunshine, rain, wind, and even snow all within a few hours. For this reason, packing layers is crucial. Layering allows you to adjust your clothing as needed throughout the day, depending on the conditions. The base layer is particularly important, as it will help to regulate your body temperature. It should be made of moisture-wicking material, such as merino wool or synthetic fabrics, which will keep sweat away from your skin and prevent you from feeling cold and damp.

Over your base layer, you'll want a mid-layer that provides insulation. Fleece jackets or wool sweaters are excellent choices, as they provide warmth without adding too much bulk. The outermost layer should be waterproof and windproof, as you will likely encounter rain or strong winds during your trip. A good-quality rain jacket and rain pants are essential, especially if you plan to spend a lot of time outdoors. Iceland's wind can be strong, particularly near coastal areas and waterfalls, so having a jacket that protects you from both wind and rain is a must.

In addition to layering your clothes, bringing the right footwear is also critical. Iceland's terrain can be challenging, with rocky paths, uneven surfaces, and slippery trails, especially near waterfalls or in rainy conditions. A sturdy pair of waterproof hiking boots is highly recommended, even if you don't plan on doing extensive hiking. The boots should provide good ankle support and have a solid grip to prevent slipping on wet or uneven ground. If you're visiting during the winter months or planning to look around glaciers or ice caves, it may also be worth packing ice cleats or spikes that can be attached to your boots for added traction.

For headgear, a warm hat that covers your ears is necessary, as even in the summer, the wind can make it feel colder than it actually is. During the winter months, a hat becomes even more important to help retain body heat. Gloves are another essential item, as your hands will need protection from the cold, especially if you're spending a lot of time outdoors. It's a good idea to bring waterproof gloves if you'll be near waterfalls or taking part in activities like glacier hiking. A scarf or neck gaiter is also useful for keeping your neck warm and shielding your face from the wind.

While Iceland's weather can be cold, particularly in the winter, the sun can still be quite strong, especially during the long daylight hours of summer. As a result, packing sunscreen is important to protect your skin from UV rays. Even on overcast days, the sun's rays can be harmful, so applying sunscreen regularly is a good habit to maintain. Sunglasses are also recommended, especially when visiting snowy areas or glaciers, where the reflection of the sun on the ice can be intense.

Another essential item for your trip to Iceland is a good-quality daypack or backpack. Whether you're going on a long hike or just exploring the towns, having a backpack allows you to carry your essentials, such as snacks, water, and extra layers of clothing. The backpack should be comfortable to wear and ideally waterproof, as this will protect your belongings from rain. If you plan on doing a lot of hiking or outdoor activities, a larger backpack with supportive straps may be more comfortable.

Speaking of water, staying hydrated is important, especially when you're spending time outdoors or hiking. Iceland has some of the cleanest water in the world, and tap water is safe to drink throughout the country. To reduce plastic waste and avoid constantly buying bottled water, it's a good idea to bring a reusable water bottle that you can refill during your trip. Many visitors to Iceland bring insulated water bottles, which keep water cold or, in colder weather, can keep drinks warm for longer periods of time.

A travel adapter is another must-have item if you're visiting Iceland from a country with different plug types. Iceland uses the European standard of 220V with two round pins, so make sure to bring an appropriate adapter if your electronics use a different type of plug. Since you may be using your phone or camera frequently to capture the stunning landscapes, it's also worth bringing a portable charger or power bank to ensure your devices don't run out of battery while you're out exploring.

For those planning on taking part in specific activities like glacier hiking, snorkeling, or horseback riding, it's important to check whether the tour companies provide specialized gear, such as wetsuits, helmets, or crampons. Many guided tours in Iceland provide this equipment, but it's always good to confirm in advance to avoid any surprises. If you're planning to spend time in one of Iceland's many geothermal pools, such as the Blue Lagoon or the Secret Lagoon, don't forget to pack a swimsuit. A quick-drying towel is also useful for visits to geothermal pools or if you're staying in accommodations that don't provide towels.

If you're visiting Iceland during the winter months or are hoping to see the Northern Lights, it's worth investing in high-quality thermal clothing. Thermal underwear, socks, and gloves will help keep you warm when temperatures drop below freezing, especially if you'll be spending time outdoors at night to catch a glimpse of the Northern Lights. A good down jacket or insulated parka is also recommended for winter travel, as it will provide warmth and protection from the cold winds.

In addition to clothing and outdoor gear, there are a few other essentials to consider when packing for Iceland. A small first aid kit is always a good idea to have on hand, especially if you're going on hikes or spending time in more remote areas. The kit should include basics like band-aids, antiseptic wipes, pain relievers, and any personal medications you may need. While Iceland has excellent healthcare services, it's always better to be prepared in case of minor injuries or illnesses.

Given the unpredictability of Iceland's weather, packing a few extra items for comfort can also make a big difference. Hand warmers can be a lifesaver on particularly cold days, especially if you're planning on being outside for extended periods. A travel umbrella might seem unnecessary in a place known for strong winds, but it can still come in handy during lighter rain showers when you're in urban areas like Reykjavík.

Lastly, consider packing items that will help you capture your experiences in Iceland. If you enjoy photography, bringing a camera with a good zoom lens is a great idea, especially for capturing distant wildlife or the vast landscapes. A tripod is useful for taking photos of the Northern Lights, as long exposure shots often produce the best results. For those who prefer to travel light, many smartphones now come with excellent cameras, so a phone with a good-quality camera may be all you need. Just make sure to bring enough memory cards or storage for all the photos and videos you'll likely be taking.

How to Get There: Transportation Options for getting to Iceland

Getting to Iceland is fairly straightforward, with the majority of visitors arriving by air, though there are some other options to consider depending on your preferences and travel plans. Iceland is an island located in the North Atlantic Ocean, so it doesn't have the same range of transportation choices as mainland European destinations. However, there are a number of reliable and accessible options that make the trip to Iceland smooth and convenient for most travelers.

The most common and practical way to get to Iceland is by flying. Iceland's main international airport, Keflavík International Airport (KEF), is located about 50 kilometers (31 miles) southwest of Reykjavík, the country's capital. Keflavík Airport is the primary point of entry for nearly all international flights to Iceland. It is well-connected to major cities across Europe, North America, and even some parts of Asia, making it accessible from many different regions around the world.

Several airlines offer direct flights to Iceland from a variety of destinations, with Icelandair and PLAY Airlines being the two primary Icelandic carriers. Icelandair operates routes from many major cities in Europe, such as London, Paris, Berlin, and Copenhagen, as well as cities in North America, including New York, Boston, Chicago, and Toronto. One of the features that makes Icelandair popular among travelers is its option to schedule a stopover in Iceland for a few days at no extra cost if you're flying between North America and Europe. This stopover option allows travelers to look around Iceland without needing to book separate flights.

In recent years, PLAY Airlines, a budget airline, has also started offering flights to Iceland from select cities in Europe and North America. While PLAY typically offers more affordable ticket prices, it's important to note that the airline operates with a low-cost model, meaning additional fees may apply for things like checked baggage, seat selection, or in-flight meals.

In addition to Icelandic airlines, several international carriers also provide direct flights to Iceland. Major airlines such as British Airways, Delta Air Lines, Lufthansa, Air Canada, and many others have regular routes to Keflavík International Airport. Depending on your location, you may be able to find a non-stop flight, or you may need to connect through another European city to reach Iceland. Layovers in cities like London, Copenhagen, or Amsterdam are common for travelers coming from North America or other distant regions.

Flight durations to Iceland vary depending on your starting point. From most European cities, direct flights to Iceland typically take around 2 to 4 hours. For travelers flying from the East Coast of the United States or Canada, the trip to Iceland usually takes about 5 to 6 hours, while flights from the West Coast may take 7 to 8 hours. Iceland's strategic location between Europe and North America makes it relatively accessible despite its remote geography.

Once you arrive at Keflavík International Airport, getting to Reykjavík and other parts of Iceland is fairly simple. The airport is well-equipped with transportation options, including buses, shuttles, taxis, and rental car services. The Flybus is a popular and convenient airport shuttle service that takes passengers directly to Reykjavík, with departures timed to coincide with incoming flights. The drive from Keflavík to Reykjavík takes around 45 minutes, and Flybus tickets can be purchased in advance or at the airport. Rental car agencies also have desks at the airport, making it easy to pick up a vehicle for those planning to look around the country by car.

While flying is by far the most popular method of getting to Iceland, there are alternative transportation options for those seeking a different experience or for travelers who prefer not to fly. One option is to travel by ferry. The Smyril Line operates a ferry service that connects Iceland with mainland Europe. The ferry, known as MS Norröna, departs from Hirtshals, Denmark, and stops in the Faroe Islands before continuing on to Iceland's eastern port of Seyðisfjörður. The trip from Denmark to Iceland takes approximately 2 to 3 days, depending on the weather conditions and stopovers. While the ferry takes significantly longer than flying, it offers a unique experience for those who want to enjoy the scenic views of the North Atlantic and stop in the Faroe Islands along the way. Traveling by ferry is particularly appealing to those who are bringing their own vehicles, as it allows travelers to transport cars, motorcycles, or campervans to Iceland. This can be an attractive option for visitors planning an extended road trip around the island, as it eliminates the need to rent a vehicle upon arrival. The ferry trip itself is comfortable, with amenities such as cabins, restaurants, and entertainment options, making it a pleasant way to start or end your Iceland adventure.

However, it's important to note that the ferry service only operates during certain times of the year, typically between April and October. Additionally, weather conditions in the North Atlantic can sometimes cause delays or rough seas, so flexibility in travel plans is advisable when choosing this option.

For those traveling from neighboring countries like the UK or other parts of Europe, another option to consider is a cruise. Several cruise lines offer routes that include Iceland as part of a longer itinerary, typically exploring the North Atlantic, Scandinavia, or the Arctic Circle. Iceland is a popular destination on cruise itineraries due to its stunning coastal landscapes and unique ports of call. Cruise ships often dock at various locations around the island, including Reykjavík, Akureyri, and Ísafjörður, allowing travelers to experience different parts of the country without the need to arrange separate transportation. While cruises offer a more leisurely way to visit Iceland, they are generally best suited for those who prefer the convenience of guided shore excursions and a more structured travel experience.

When deciding on how to get to Iceland, it's essential to consider factors such as budget, time, and personal preferences. For most travelers, flying will be the fastest and most convenient way to reach the island, with a wide range of flight options available throughout the year. However, for those with more time or a desire for a unique travel experience, ferries or cruises can offer an alternative route that adds an extra element of adventure to the trip.

Regardless of how you choose to get there, arriving in Iceland is the first step in what will undoubtedly be an unforgettable experience. Iceland's natural beauty, friendly locals, and wide range of activities make it a destination worth exploring, and whether you arrive by plane, ferry, or cruise, the trip will only add to the excitement of find outing all that Iceland has to offer.

CHAPTER 2

GETTING AROUND ICELAND

How to Get Around

Getting around Iceland can be a truly rewarding part of your trip, as the country is filled with natural wonders, and exploring these stunning landscapes often requires some level of travel between towns, rural areas, and various points of interest. Unlike many other European countries, Iceland does not have a dense public transportation system, so it is important to plan how you will move around during your visit. Fortunately, there are several transportation options available, each with its own advantages depending on your preferences, budget, and the type of experience you are looking for.

Car Rental

One of the most popular and practical ways to get around Iceland is by renting a car. Renting a car gives you the freedom and flexibility to look around the country at your own pace, especially if you plan to visit many of the more remote or off-the-beaten-path attractions. The vast majority of tourists who visit Iceland choose to rent a car, and there are numerous rental car companies available, both international and local, with offices at Keflavík International Airport as well as in Reykjavík and other towns. Rental car options range from small economy cars to larger SUVs and 4x4 vehicles, which are essential if you plan on exploring Iceland's highland areas or traveling during the winter months when road conditions can be challenging.

Driving in Iceland is relatively straightforward, especially along the Ring Road (Route 1), which circles the island and connects most of the country's main attractions and towns. The Ring Road is well-maintained and paved, making it easy for tourists to find your way, even if they are unfamiliar with the country. Many of Iceland's most famous natural sites, such as waterfalls, glaciers, and hot springs, are located along or near the Ring Road, making it a convenient route for visitors. However, if you plan to venture into Iceland's interior, particularly the highlands or more remote areas, you will encounter gravel roads, which may require a 4x4 vehicle for safety and comfort. It is important to be aware of road conditions before setting out, as weather and terrain can change quickly, especially during the winter months when some roads may be closed due to snow or ice.

When renting a car in Iceland, there are a few important factors to consider. First, make sure to check what is included in the rental agreement, especially in terms of insurance coverage. Iceland's rugged terrain can be tough on vehicles, and even paved roads can present hazards such as loose gravel, volcanic ash, or strong winds that can damage the car. Many rental companies offer additional insurance options, such as gravel protection or sand and ash protection, which may be worth considering depending on where you plan to travel. Additionally, if you plan to visit during the winter, you'll want to ensure that your rental car is equipped with winter tires, as this is required by law in Iceland from November to April.

Another important aspect of driving in Iceland is understanding the local rules of the road. Icelanders drive on the right side of the road, and the speed limit is generally 90 km/h (56 mph) on paved rural roads, 80 km/h (50 mph) on gravel roads, and 50 km/h (31 mph) in urban areas. Speed cameras are common throughout the country, so it's important to obey the speed limits. Additionally, seatbelts are mandatory for all passengers, and driving under the influence of alcohol is strictly prohibited. Iceland also has many single-lane bridges in rural areas, and the general rule is that the vehicle closest to the bridge has the right of way. If you are unfamiliar with driving in winter conditions, it's a good idea to research tips on driving in snow and ice before your trip to ensure your safety.

Tour buses

While renting a car is a great option for many travelers, it's not the only way to get around Iceland. For those who prefer not to drive or want to leave the logistics to someone else, joining guided tours is a popular alternative. Tour companies in Iceland offer a wide range of excursions that take visitors to the country's most famous attractions as well as more hidden gems. These tours are especially popular for travelers who want to visit places like the Golden Circle, the South Coast, or the Snæfellsnes Peninsula, as they provide transportation and a knowledgeable guide to enhance the experience. Many tours are available in Reykjavík, and they range from day trips to multi-day adventures that cover different parts of the country.

Tour buses are a comfortable and convenient way to look around Iceland, especially for visitors who may not feel confident driving in unfamiliar conditions. In addition to sightseeing tours, there are also bus services that operate on popular routes between towns and tourist sites. These buses, often referred to as "Icelandic buses" or "long-distance buses," are run by companies such as Strætó and Reykjavík Excursions. They provide scheduled services between Reykjavík and other regions, including popular tourist destinations like Akureyri, the Westfjords, and the Eastfjords. While this option doesn't offer the same level of flexibility as renting a car, it is a good choice for budget-conscious travelers who want to look around Iceland without the responsibility of driving.

For those looking for a more sustainable and eco-friendly way to look around Iceland, cycling is another option to consider. While not the most common mode of transportation, especially given Iceland's often harsh weather conditions, cycling around the country is an option for adventurous travelers. Some tourists opt to cycle part or all of the Ring Road during the summer months, when weather conditions are more favorable. If you're not planning to cycle the entire island, there are also several short cycling routes that allow you to look around scenic areas near towns and cities. Bike rentals are available in Reykjavík and other larger towns, and some tourists even bring their own bikes if they are planning a longer cycling trip. Keep in mind that cycling in Iceland can be challenging due to the country's strong winds, and it is important to be well-prepared with proper gear and an understanding of the route.

Buses and Taxi's

In addition to buses, taxis are available in most urban areas, particularly in Reykjavík. However, taxi services in Iceland can be expensive compared to other countries, so they are generally not the most cost-effective option for long-distance travel. Taxis are best used for short trips within cities or for getting to and from the airport if you prefer not to use a bus or shuttle service. For tourists staying in Reykjavík, walking is also a great way to get around the city center, as many of the main attractions are within walking distance of each other.

If you prefer the convenience of booking rides on your phone, local transportation apps like Hreyfill are available for ordering taxis. However, it's worth noting that international ride-sharing services like Uber and Lyft are not currently available in Iceland, so taxis or private transfers are the primary option for short, on-demand trips.

For those visiting more remote areas or staying in rural accommodations, renting a car or booking guided tours is usually the best way to ensure you can reach your destination. Public transportation options become more limited the farther you get from the capital and main tourist routes, so it's important to plan ahead if you're visiting areas like the Westfjords, the Eastfjords, or the highlands.

Public Transportation

Public transportation in Iceland is limited compared to many other European countries, but it is still a viable option for tourists who prefer not to drive or for those looking for more affordable ways to get around the country. While Iceland does not have an extensive train system or metro networks like you might find in larger cities, it does offer bus services that connect the capital city, Reykjavík, to other towns and regions. If you plan on using public transport, it's essential to know what options are available, how they operate, and how you can make the most of them during your stay in Iceland.

One of the main providers of public bus services in Iceland is Strætó, which operates the local and regional buses throughout the country. Strætó runs a network of buses in the Greater Reykjavík area, providing reliable public transportation within the capital city and its surrounding towns. This makes it easy for visitors staying in Reykjavík to get around without needing a car, especially if you plan to look around the city's downtown area, visit nearby suburbs, or head out to attractions like the Blue Lagoon or the Perlan Museum. The buses in Reykjavík are generally well-maintained, clean, and comfortable, making them a good option for both locals and tourists.

Strætó buses in Reykjavík run frequently during the weekdays, with slightly reduced services on weekends and public holidays. The schedules are relatively easy to follow, with buses arriving at regular intervals. If you are staying in Reykjavík, you will likely find that the bus system provides convenient access to most of the major sights and districts. For tourists, the Reykjavík City Card offers unlimited access to Strætó buses within the capital area, in addition to free admission to several museums and other attractions. This can be a cost-effective option if you plan on using public transport frequently during your stay in the city.

While the bus system in Reykjavík is reliable for local travel, the options for getting beyond the capital and into the countryside or remote areas of Iceland are more limited. Strætó also operates long-distance bus routes that connect Reykjavík to other regions of the country. These buses can be a convenient way to travel between major towns, such as Akureyri in the north or Ísafjörður in the Westfjords, but the routes are not as frequent as those within the city. Some long-distance buses may only run once or twice a day, depending on the time of year, and certain routes may be reduced or even suspended during the winter months due to weather conditions. It's important to plan ahead if you're relying on these services, as missing a bus can mean waiting until the next day for another one.

For tourists who want to visit Iceland's famous natural landmarks and tourist attractions outside of Reykjavík, there are several bus companies that offer organized tours and shuttle services to popular destinations. Reykjavík Excursions and Gray Line Iceland are two well-known companies that operate scheduled bus services to major tourist sites, such as the Golden Circle, the Blue Lagoon, and the South Coast. These buses are designed with tourists in mind, often including commentary or guides who provide information about the sites you'll visit along the way. While these services are not strictly part of the public transportation system, they offer an alternative for those who want to look around Iceland without renting a car.

If you plan to travel between towns and more rural areas, it's worth noting that the bus services can be infrequent and may not always align with your schedule, especially if you are visiting during the off-season. Some routes may only operate during the summer months when there are more tourists, while others may be less frequent or suspended in the winter due to icy road conditions or snow. Additionally, many rural bus stops are located on the outskirts of small towns, so you may need to walk or arrange for a taxi to get to your final destination if your accommodation is not close to the stop.

Another challenge with public transportation in Iceland is the lack of services that connect to some of the country's more remote regions, particularly the highlands and interior areas. These regions are often only accessible by specialized 4x4 vehicles due to the rugged terrain and gravel roads, so public buses do not typically operate in these areas. If you are hoping to look around the highlands, visit volcanic landscapes, or reach more isolated hiking trails, public buses will not take you there, and you may need to consider guided tours, rental vehicles, or private transport services.

While public buses in Iceland are relatively straightforward to use, it's helpful to know a few key details about how they operate. Tickets for Strætó buses can be purchased either in advance or directly from the driver when you board the bus.

If you choose to pay in cash, make sure you have the exact fare, as drivers typically do not carry change. Another option for purchasing tickets is to use the Strætó app, which allows you to buy single tickets or day passes directly on your smartphone. The app is available in English and can be downloaded for free, making it a convenient option for tourists. You can also use the app to check bus schedules and plan your route in advance, which is especially helpful for long-distance travel.

Public transportation in Iceland also includes domestic flights for those who want to travel longer distances quickly. Although flights are not part of the bus network, they provide another way to get around the country if you're traveling between major towns or cities. Icelandair and Air Iceland Connect operate domestic flights from Reykjavík's domestic airport, with routes to towns such as Akureyri, Egilsstaðir, and Ísafjörður. While flying is generally faster than taking a bus for long distances, it is also more expensive and may not be necessary for travelers who prefer to experience Iceland's landscapes by road.

Local Transportation Apps

Getting around Iceland can be greatly simplified with the help of local transportation apps, which are designed to make travel more convenient and accessible for both locals and tourists. Although Iceland does not have a large or extensive public transportation system, there are several key apps that can help you find your way the country, find transportation, and manage your trip efficiently. These apps cover a range of services, including buses, taxis, and even car rentals, making it easier to plan trips, check schedules, and book rides as needed.

One of the most important transportation apps in Iceland is the Strætó app. This app is primarily used for the public bus system, which operates within the Reykjavík area and also connects the capital with other towns and regions across the country. The Strætó app is essential for anyone planning to use the bus network, as it allows you to buy tickets, check bus schedules, and plan your route all in one place. The app is available for both Android and iOS devices, and it is designed to be user-friendly, with clear instructions and options for English speakers.

The Strætó app offers a number of useful features for travelers. For instance, you can use the app to purchase single bus tickets, day passes, or longer-term passes if you plan on using the bus frequently. Once you purchase a ticket through the app, it is stored digitally on your phone, and you simply need to show it to the driver when boarding the bus. This eliminates the need to carry cash or worry about exact change, making it a convenient option for tourists who may not be familiar with the local currency or payment methods.

Additionally, the Strætó app provides real-time information about bus schedules and routes. This is especially helpful in a country like Iceland, where weather conditions can sometimes affect transportation. The app allows you to see when the next bus is arriving, check for any delays, and plan your route based on the most up-to-date information. For tourists who may not be familiar with the bus routes, the app also includes a trip planner feature, which allows you to input your starting point and destination to receive step-by-step directions on which buses to take and where to transfer. This can be particularly helpful when navigating between different towns or visiting more remote areas where bus services may be less frequent.

In addition to buses, taxis are a common form of transportation in Iceland, especially within cities like Reykjavík. While ride-sharing services like Uber and Lyft do not operate in Iceland, there are local taxi services that you can access through transportation apps. One of the most widely used taxi apps in Iceland is Hreyfill. The Hreyfill app allows users to book taxis quickly and easily, either for immediate rides or for scheduled pickups at a specific time. Like the Strætó app, Hreyfill is available in English, making it accessible for tourists who may not speak Icelandic.

The Hreyfill app offers several features that enhance the convenience of using taxis in Iceland. You can use the app to track the location of your taxi in real-time, ensuring that you know exactly when your driver will arrive. This is particularly useful in busy areas or during bad weather when it may be difficult to spot your taxi from a distance. The app also allows you to enter your destination in advance, so the driver knows where you're headed as soon as they pick you up. This can be a great time-saver, especially if you're visiting a place with an unfamiliar name or spelling. Additionally, the app provides an estimate of the fare for your trip, so you can have a general idea of the cost before you get in the taxi.

If you're planning to travel outside of the capital or look around Iceland's natural wonders, renting a car may be the best option for getting around. Several apps are available that make the car rental process easier and more streamlined. One such app is Blue Car Rental, which offers a range of rental vehicles suited for Iceland's unique driving conditions. The app allows you to book a car in advance, choose from different types of vehicles (such as economy cars, SUVs, or 4x4 vehicles), and arrange for pickup and drop-off at convenient locations, including Keflavík International Airport.

The Blue Car Rental app also provides useful information about Iceland's road conditions and driving rules, which is important for tourists who may not be familiar with the country's terrain. Iceland's weather can change rapidly, and some roads, especially in the highlands, require 4x4 vehicles or are closed during certain times of the year. The app includes tips for safe driving in Iceland, as well as information about the insurance options available for rental cars. This can help you feel more confident and prepared as you look around Iceland by car.

Another useful app for car rentals in Iceland is SADcars, which offers budget-friendly rental options for travelers looking to look around the island at their own pace. Like Blue Car Rental, the SADcars app allows you to browse different types of vehicles, make a reservation, and check availability at various rental locations. The app is designed to be simple and straightforward, making it easy to rent a car even if you've never rented one before. It also includes information on the best routes to take and places to visit, helping you make the most of your road trip in Iceland.

For tourists who prefer a more eco-friendly option, Green Motion is a car rental service that specializes in environmentally friendly vehicles, such as electric cars and hybrids. The Green Motion app allows you to reserve these vehicles, providing a sustainable option for getting around Iceland. Electric vehicle charging stations are becoming more common across the country, particularly in Reykjavík and along major tourist routes, making it easier to look around Iceland in an eco-conscious way. The app includes a map of charging stations and information on how to use them, making it a practical choice for travelers who are concerned about their environmental impact.

In addition to these transportation-specific apps, there are a few other apps that can be helpful when getting around Iceland. One example is the 112 Iceland app, which is an emergency app that allows you to contact Iceland's emergency services quickly and easily. While not a transportation app in the traditional sense, it is an important tool to have if you're traveling in more remote areas or going on outdoor adventures like hiking or glacier tours. The app allows you to send your location to emergency responders if you need help, which can be crucial in Iceland's wilderness where cellphone reception may be limited.

Bike Rentals and Cycling Routes

Cycling in Iceland offers a unique and rewarding way to look around the country's landscapes, from its vibrant cities to its remote, rugged wilderness. Bike rentals are a popular option for tourists who want to experience Iceland at a slower pace, enjoying the fresh air and incredible scenery that the country has to offer. Whether you're interested in cycling through Reykjavík's urban streets or starting on a long-distance trip around the island, biking provides a flexible and eco-friendly transportation option.

If you're staying in Reykjavík or visiting other towns, renting a bike is straightforward and accessible. Several bike rental companies operate in the capital, making it easy for tourists to pick up a bicycle for a few hours, a day, or even longer. Bike rentals are available for all types of cyclists, whether you're looking for a basic city bike, a mountain bike for rougher terrain, or an electric bike to make the ride a little easier. The rental shops provide helmets, locks, and sometimes other accessories like panniers or bike racks, ensuring that you have everything you need for a safe and enjoyable ride.

Reykjavík is particularly bike-friendly, with a network of cycling paths that allow visitors to look around the city comfortably and safely. Many of the city's main attractions, such as the Hallgrímskirkja Church, Harpa Concert Hall, and the Sun Voyager sculpture, are easily accessible by bike. Cycling along the coastline provides stunning views of the ocean, and the paths are well-maintained, making it a smooth ride for both locals and tourists. The city also has dedicated bike lanes on some of the roads, which helps to reduce interactions with motor traffic and create a more relaxed cycling experience.

If you're interested in exploring Reykjavík's parks and green spaces, cycling is an ideal way to get around. The popular Elliðaárdalur Valley, located in the eastern part of the city, is a scenic area with trails that wind through forests, along rivers, and past small waterfalls. Cyclists can enjoy the peaceful surroundings while staying close to the city. Other parks, such as Laugardalur, are also easily accessible by bike, providing opportunities to look around Iceland's natural beauty without leaving the capital.

Beyond Reykjavík, there are plenty of cycling routes that take you through Iceland's extraordinary landscapes. One of the most famous cycling routes is the Ring Road, also known as Route 1, which circles the entire island. Cycling the Ring Road is a bucket-list adventure for many avid cyclists, offering an unforgettable trip through diverse environments, from volcanic deserts and towering waterfalls to glaciers and geothermal areas. The full route is about 1,332 kilometers (828 miles) long, and while it can be challenging, it's a once-in-a-lifetime experience for those who are well-prepared.

Cycling the Ring Road requires careful planning and preparation. The weather in Iceland can change rapidly, and strong winds, rain, and cold temperatures are common even in the summer months. It's important to bring the right gear, including waterproof clothing, layers to keep warm, and sturdy equipment that can handle Iceland's sometimes rough roads. Most cyclists who take on the Ring Road choose to do so during the summer, when the weather is more stable, and daylight lasts almost 24 hours. This gives you more time to cycle each day and reduces the risk of traveling in the dark, which is important given that many sections of the Ring Road are remote, with few towns or services.

In addition to the Ring Road, there are other scenic routes that are well-suited for cycling. The Westfjords region, known for its dramatic fjords and remote beauty, offers challenging but rewarding cycling opportunities. The roads in this area are less busy than the Ring Road, but they can be steeper and more difficult due to the mountainous terrain. However, the payoff is spectacular views and a sense of solitude that is hard to find in more popular tourist areas.

The Snæfellsnes Peninsula is another great destination for cyclists. Often referred to as "Iceland in miniature" because of its diverse landscapes, Snæfellsnes offers a mix of lava fields, beaches, cliffs, and mountains, all within a relatively compact area. Cycling around the peninsula gives you the chance to experience everything from black sand beaches to the iconic Snæfellsjökull glacier. The roads on the peninsula are generally quiet and manageable for cyclists, though it's still important to be prepared for strong winds, especially along the coast.

If you're new to cycling or prefer shorter rides, there are many opportunities for day trips and half-day rides throughout the country. Some tourists enjoy renting bikes to look around areas like Þingvellir National Park, which is part of the Golden Circle and offers stunning landscapes and historical significance. The park's trails are well-marked, and the terrain is relatively flat, making it an accessible option for cyclists of all levels. You can cycle through the rift valley between the North American and Eurasian tectonic plates, which is a fascinating geological feature unique to Iceland.

For those who want an easier ride, electric bike rentals are becoming increasingly popular in Iceland. E-bikes provide motorized assistance, making it less physically demanding to cycle over long distances or uphill. This can be especially useful for tourists who want to enjoy the landscapes without the physical strain of traditional cycling. E-bikes are available for rent in Reykjavík and some other towns, and they are a great option for exploring the city or going on shorter rides through the countryside.

Another consideration when cycling in Iceland is safety. The roads in Iceland, especially outside of Reykjavík, can be narrow, and many are not designed with cyclists in mind. While Iceland's drivers are generally courteous to cyclists, it's important to stay alert and visible on the roads. Wearing high-visibility clothing and using lights on your bike can help ensure that drivers see you, especially during low-light conditions or in bad weather. It's also essential to follow the rules of the road, including cycling on the right side and signaling your turns.

If you're planning to cycle in more remote areas or on gravel roads, it's a good idea to bring a repair kit with you, as services can be limited outside of the major towns. Flat tires or other mechanical issues can happen, especially on Iceland's rougher terrain, so being able to fix your bike on the go is important. In more popular areas, such as Reykjavík or along the Ring Road, there are bike shops and rental companies that can assist with repairs, but it's always better to be prepared.

Cycling in Iceland is not only an eco-friendly way to travel, but it also offers an intimate connection with the natural environment. The slower pace of cycling allows you to take in the sights, sounds, and smells of Iceland's wilderness in a way that you can't experience from a car or bus. Whether you're cycling through green valleys, along rugged coastlines, or past bubbling geothermal springs, the sense of freedom and adventure that comes with biking in Iceland is unmatched.

Transportation for Remote Areas

Transportation in remote areas of Iceland is a unique challenge due to the country's vast, rugged terrain and often unpredictable weather conditions. While Iceland's more populated areas, such as Reykjavík and the Ring Road that circles the island, offer reliable options for getting around, traveling to remote regions like the highlands, the Westfjords, or parts of the Eastfjords requires careful planning and a different approach. These areas, though more isolated, offer some of the most breathtaking natural beauty in the country, from untouched landscapes to dramatic fjords and remote wilderness. Getting to these places is not always easy, but the effort is more than worth it.

One of the most important considerations when traveling to remote areas in Iceland is the type of vehicle you use. In many cases, regular cars are not suitable for the rough terrain you'll encounter in these parts of the country. While a two-wheel-drive vehicle is fine for driving the Ring Road or visiting towns and cities, a four-wheel-drive (4x4) vehicle is essential for accessing many of Iceland's more isolated areas. This is particularly true if you plan to visit the highlands or travel on F-roads, which are mountain roads that are unpaved, often narrow, and can be quite challenging. These roads are marked with an "F" before the number and are typically open only during the summer months, usually from June to September, depending on the weather and road conditions. F-roads are often rocky, steep, and sometimes require crossing rivers, so a 4x4 vehicle is necessary not only for comfort but also for safety.

If you're renting a vehicle for your trip to Iceland, it's essential to check with the rental company to ensure that your car is equipped to handle these kinds of conditions. Many rental companies offer 4x4 vehicles specifically designed for off-road driving, and some even provide extra equipment such as spare tires, tire repair kits, and GPS navigation systems that can be helpful in remote areas where road signs or cellular signals may be limited. It's also worth noting that driving on F-roads without the proper vehicle can void your rental agreement, so it's important to choose the right car from the start.

In addition to needing a suitable vehicle, it's crucial to be aware of the road conditions before heading into remote areas. The Icelandic Road and Coastal Administration provides regular updates on road conditions across the country, including information on which roads are open, closed, or potentially dangerous due to weather or other factors. This information is available online, and it's highly recommended to check it regularly, especially if you're planning to drive in remote regions. The roads in these areas can be affected by sudden changes in weather, from heavy rain to snow or fog, which can make driving difficult or even impossible at times. River crossings are also a common feature on F-roads, and these can be particularly hazardous after heavy rain or snowmelt, so it's important to assess the depth and current before attempting to cross.

For those who prefer not to drive or are uncomfortable with the challenges of navigating remote areas, guided tours are another option. Many tour companies in Iceland offer specialized trips to the highlands, the Westfjords, and other remote regions, often using modified vehicles that are designed for tough terrain. These tours can be a great way to experience Iceland's more isolated beauty without the stress of having to drive yourself. The guides on these tours are often experienced in off-road driving and familiar with the conditions in these areas, ensuring a safer and more informed trip. These tours can range from day trips to multi-day expeditions, depending on how much of the remote areas you want to look around.

If you plan to visit the highlands, which include some of Iceland's most famous natural landmarks like Landmannalaugar and Askja, a 4x4 vehicle or a guided tour is the best way to get there. The highlands are a vast, uninhabited area in the center of the island, and while the scenery is breathtaking, with volcanic deserts, geothermal hot springs, and glaciers, the terrain can be difficult to find your way. In addition to rough roads and river crossings, the highlands are also more exposed to the elements, with little shelter from wind, rain, or cold temperatures. Even in the summer, conditions can be harsh, so it's important to be prepared with the right clothing, equipment, and transportation.

The Westfjords, located in the northwestern part of Iceland, are another remote region that requires careful planning when it comes to transportation. The roads in the Westfjords are often steep and winding, with many sections running along the edges of cliffs or fjords. While a 4x4 vehicle is not always necessary for driving in this region, it can be helpful, especially if you plan to visit more isolated areas or if you're traveling during the winter when snow and ice can make the roads more difficult to find your way. The Westfjords are one of the least populated areas of Iceland, and while the lack of crowds makes it a peaceful place to look around, it also means that services like gas stations, restaurants, and accommodations are more spread out. It's important to plan your route carefully, ensuring that you have enough fuel and supplies for the trip.

Public transportation options are limited in remote areas of Iceland, especially compared to the more developed routes around Reykjavík and the southern part of the island. While long-distance buses do connect some of the larger towns, such as Ísafjörður in the Westfjords or Akureyri in the north, they do not cover the more isolated regions, and their schedules may be infrequent, especially in the winter. If you're relying on public transport to reach a remote destination, you may need to combine it with other forms of transportation, such as hiking, biking, or taking a taxi for the last leg of the trip. However, public transportation is generally not a practical option for exploring the more remote wilderness areas of Iceland.

One additional form of transportation that can be useful in remote areas is domestic flights. Iceland has several domestic airports, including ones in the Westfjords and northern regions, such as Ísafjörður and Akureyri. Air Iceland Connect and other local airlines offer flights between Reykjavík and these more distant towns, which can be a convenient way to cut down on travel time if you're planning to visit both urban and remote areas. While flights won't take you into the heart of the highlands or other wilderness areas, they can be a good starting point for further exploration by car or guided tour.

For those interested in adventure travel, cycling and hiking are also popular ways to look around remote areas of Iceland. While cycling in the highlands or along rough roads can be physically demanding, it offers an up-close experience of the natural landscape. Cyclists need to be well-prepared, with sturdy bikes and proper gear, as the weather and road conditions can be harsh. Many adventurers choose to cycle the Ring Road, but more intrepid travelers venture off the main roads to look around less-visited areas. Similarly, hiking offers the chance to experience Iceland's untouched wilderness, though it requires careful planning and an understanding of the terrain. There are several long-distance hiking trails in the highlands, and many of them require crossing rivers or navigating challenging paths, so it's important to be physically fit and properly equipped.

CHAPTER 3

PRACTICAL TRAVEL TIPS

Currency exchange in Iceland is a straightforward process, but it's helpful to understand the best places and options available to exchange money as a tourist. The official currency of Iceland is the Icelandic króna (ISK), and while Iceland is known for being a largely cashless society, there are still some instances where you may need to exchange or withdraw physical currency.

One of the easiest places to exchange currency in Iceland is upon arrival at Keflavík International Airport. The airport houses several currency exchange counters and ATMs, making it convenient for travelers to get local currency as soon as they land. One of the most common services available at the airport is Arion Bank's exchange desk, which allows travelers to exchange major currencies like US dollars, euros, and British pounds for Icelandic krónur. The airport also has ATMs where you can withdraw Icelandic krónur directly using your debit or credit card. Using an ATM can be a more cost-effective way to obtain cash, as the rates at currency exchange counters can sometimes include higher fees or less favorable exchange rates.

If you plan to exchange currency at the airport, it's a good idea to do a small exchange initially, just to cover any immediate expenses such as transportation or snacks. While the convenience of airport exchange services is undeniable, the rates you receive at the airport may not be as competitive as those offered by banks in the city. It's often better to exchange only a small amount at the airport and then seek out better rates at a bank or ATM once you've arrived in Reykjavík or other towns.

Reykjavík, Iceland's capital, offers several locations where you can exchange currency. The main banks in Iceland— Arion Bank, Landsbankinn, and Íslandsbanki—all offer currency exchange services at their branches throughout the city. These banks typically offer better exchange rates compared to airport counters or currency exchange kiosks. It's advisable to visit a bank branch during normal banking hours (usually from 9 AM to 4 PM on weekdays) if you need to exchange currency. You will need to bring identification, such as a passport, when exchanging money at a bank.

ATMs, or "hraðbanki" in Icelandic, are widely available in Reykjavík and other larger towns. Using an ATM is one of the most convenient ways to access Icelandic krónur, especially since most travelers can simply use their debit or credit cards to withdraw cash. Most ATMs in Iceland allow you to select English as the language of the transaction, making it easy for tourists to use. Additionally, Icelandic ATMs typically accept a range of international debit and credit cards, including those from major networks like Visa, Mastercard, and sometimes American Express. If you plan to use an ATM to withdraw money, it's important to check with your bank beforehand to understand any foreign transaction fees or ATM withdrawal fees that may apply.

One of the benefits of using ATMs in Iceland is that they offer competitive exchange rates, often closely aligned with the official rates set by the banks. This means that withdrawing cash from an ATM can be a more cost-effective option than exchanging cash at a currency counter. However, it's a good idea to withdraw larger amounts at once to minimize any flat fees that your bank may charge for international withdrawals. Most ATMs in Iceland allow you to withdraw up to 100,000 ISK per transaction, though this limit may vary depending on the specific ATM or the terms set by your bank.

In addition to banks and ATMs, there are also several currency exchange kiosks available in Reykjavík. While these kiosks can be convenient, especially if you're in the city center and don't want to visit a bank, they often charge higher fees or offer less favorable exchange rates compared to banks or ATMs. If you choose to use a currency exchange kiosk, be sure to compare the rates with those offered at a bank or ATM beforehand. Some kiosks also charge service fees, which can make a noticeable difference in the overall amount you receive after the exchange.

While it's good to be aware of where and how to exchange money in Iceland, it's important to note that Iceland is a largely cashless society. Most businesses, including hotels, restaurants, shops, and even taxis, accept credit and debit cards for transactions. In fact, many locals rarely use cash at all. This makes traveling in Iceland very convenient for tourists, as you can pay for almost everything with a card. Visa and Mastercard are the most widely accepted cards, and many businesses also accept American Express, though it's not as universal. Contactless payments, such as using Apple Pay or Google Pay, are also commonly accepted, especially in larger cities and tourist areas.

Given Iceland's preference for card payments, it's possible to travel through most of the country without needing much cash at all. However, there are still some situations where having cash on hand may be useful. For instance, in more remote areas or small towns, some smaller businesses, local markets, or family-run guesthouses may prefer cash payments, especially if they do not have card readers. In these cases, having some Icelandic krónur can save you the hassle of searching for an ATM. Public restroom in certain rural areas may also require a small fee, which is sometimes easier to pay in cash. Additionally, some parking meters in Reykjavík and other cities may not accept card payments, so having a small amount of cash can be helpful for paying parking fees.

If you need to exchange currency in smaller towns or rural areas, the options may be more limited compared to Reykjavík. While most towns will have at least one bank or ATM where you can withdraw or exchange currency, it's important to plan ahead, especially if you're traveling to remote areas where services can be sparse. Some regions, like the highlands or the Westfjords, may not have ATMs readily available, so it's a good idea to withdraw or exchange enough cash before heading into these areas. If you're staying in a remote part of the country, ask your accommodation provider in advance about the nearest place to withdraw or exchange money.

For tourists planning to exchange money in Iceland, it's also important to be aware of any restrictions or requirements. While there are no strict limits on how much foreign currency you can exchange, large transactions may require additional documentation, such as proof of where the money is coming from or a reason for the exchange. This is more likely to be an issue for very large sums of money, rather than typical amounts exchanged by tourists.

Finally, it's worth noting that Iceland's currency exchange rates can fluctuate, so it's a good idea to keep an eye on the rates before your trip. While you may not be able to predict the best time to exchange currency perfectly, being aware of the current rates can help you make informed decisions about when and where to exchange your money. Many online platforms allow you to check the latest exchange rates, and some even offer rate alerts if you're looking to exchange a larger amount.

Electricity and Plug Adapters

When visiting Iceland, understanding the electricity system and the need for plug adapters is important to ensure that you can use and charge your electronic devices without any trouble. Iceland's electrical system is similar to many other European countries, but if you're coming from North

America, the United Kingdom, or other regions where the voltage and plug types differ, it's essential to know what kind of adapter or converter you might need.

Iceland operates on a 230-volt electrical system with a frequency of 50 hertz (Hz). This is the standard voltage used in most European countries, including Germany, France, and Spain. If you are traveling from a country where the voltage is lower, such as the United States or Canada, where the voltage is typically 120 volts, your electronic devices may not be compatible with Iceland's electrical outlets unless they are dual voltage. Fortunately, many modern electronic devices, such as laptops, smartphones, and cameras, are designed to handle a range of voltages. You can check the label on your device's power adapter or charger to see if it supports 230 volts. If it says something like "Input: 100-240V," your device can be used in Iceland without needing a voltage converter.

However, even if your devices are compatible with Iceland's voltage, you will still need to consider the plug type. Iceland uses Type C and Type F plugs, which have two round pins. Type C plugs are the most common and are used in many European countries. They are simple, with two round pins that fit into the outlets in Iceland. Type F plugs are similar to Type C, but they are slightly larger and also include grounding clips on the sides. Both plug types work with Iceland's electrical outlets, and you'll likely encounter both styles during your stay. If you are traveling from a country that uses different plug types, such as the UK with its Type G plugs or North America with its flat pin Type A and Type

B plugs, you will need a plug adapter to connect your devices to Iceland's outlets.

Plug adapters are simple devices that allow your plugs to fit into the outlets in another country. They don't convert voltage, so it's important to make sure your devices are dual voltage before using them. Plug adapters can be purchased before your trip at most electronics stores, online retailers, or even at the airport. If you forget to bring one, they are also available for purchase in Iceland, though they may be more expensive, especially in tourist areas. It's a good idea to buy a universal plug adapter, which is designed to work in multiple countries, including Iceland. These adapters often come with interchangeable plug heads, so you can use them for future trips to other regions as well.

If you have devices that are not dual voltage, such as certain hair dryers, electric razors, or older electronics, you may also need a voltage converter in addition to a plug adapter. A voltage converter changes the electricity coming from the outlet into the correct voltage for your device. Converters are typically larger than simple plug adapters and can be more cumbersome to carry. For this reason, many travelers prefer to leave high-power devices like hair dryers at home and instead use dual voltage travel versions or rely on the amenities provided by their accommodation.

It's also worth noting that Iceland's electricity system is very reliable, even in remote areas. Thanks to the country's use of renewable energy sources, particularly geothermal and hydroelectric power, Iceland has one of the cleanest and most consistent electricity supplies in the world. Blackouts or power outages are rare, even in the most isolated parts of the island, so you can feel confident that your devices will stay charged throughout your trip.

For tourists bringing several devices, it's helpful to carry a power strip or multi-plug adapter with you. Many hotels and guesthouses in Iceland have limited outlets in their rooms, and having a power strip allows you to charge multiple devices at once without needing to switch between plugs. Just be sure that your power strip is compatible with 230 volts and has the correct plug adapter for Iceland.

If you're planning to spend time in more rural areas of Iceland, such as the highlands or the Westfjords, or if you're starting on a camping or hiking trip, it's important to consider how you'll keep your devices charged when you're away from traditional power sources. Portable power banks are a useful item to bring, as they allow you to charge your phone, camera, or other small devices when you don't have access to an outlet. Some power banks come with solar charging capabilities, which can be particularly useful during the long daylight hours of summer in Iceland. If you're driving a rental car, many vehicles come equipped with USB ports or 12V sockets where you can charge your devices while on the road.

For those who are particularly concerned about running out of power, renting or purchasing a portable solar charger or power generator is another option. These devices are designed for outdoor use and can keep your electronics charged even when you're in the most remote parts of Iceland. While these may not be necessary for most tourists staying in hotels or guesthouses, they can be a valuable addition to your gear if you're planning a longer trip in Iceland's wilderness.

When packing for your trip to Iceland, it's also a good idea to bring a small adapter or converter for any medical devices you may need to use. CPAP machines, insulin pumps, and other portable medical equipment often require electricity to operate, and ensuring that you have the correct adapter and voltage converter, if needed, will give you peace of mind while traveling.

Internet and Communication

When traveling to Iceland, having access to reliable internet and communication services is essential for most tourists. Whether you want to stay connected with family and friends, find your way the country's breathtaking landscapes, or simply look up restaurant recommendations, having access to the internet and a dependable communication system will make your trip much more convenient. Iceland, despite its rugged and sometimes remote geography, boasts excellent communication infrastructure, with high-speed internet widely available and mobile coverage extending to most parts of the country. Understanding how to access these services during your trip will help ensure that you can stay connected when you need it.

First and foremost, Iceland has one of the best internet networks in the world, especially for a country with such a small population and large rural areas. High-speed internet is widely available throughout the country, particularly in urban areas like Reykjavík, Akureyri, and other larger towns. Most hotels, guesthouses, hostels, and even campgrounds offer free Wi-Fi to guests. The Wi-Fi speeds are typically fast and reliable, making it easy to use your phone, laptop, or tablet for streaming, video calls, or browsing the web without any significant interruptions. Even in smaller guesthouses in more rural areas, it is common to find Wi-Fi available for guests, although the speed may be slower compared to that in the cities. However, considering Iceland's remote location in the North Atlantic, the quality of the internet is remarkably good.

If you are staying in a major city like Reykjavík, you'll find free public Wi-Fi available in many public spaces, cafes, restaurants, and libraries. Reykjavík, in particular, is known for being a tech-savvy city, and tourists can easily connect to the internet in most parts of the city without needing to use mobile data. Coffee shops, restaurants, and even some museums offer free Wi-Fi to their customers, which makes it convenient for travelers to stay connected without incurring additional costs. Shopping malls, bus stations, and other public buildings often provide free Wi-Fi as well. As a tourist, this means that you can often rely on these free networks for checking maps, looking up directions, or sending messages without needing to worry about data usage.

However, if you plan to travel outside of the city into more remote areas, such as the highlands, the Westfjords, or the countryside, Wi-Fi may not always be readily available. While some guesthouses, farms, or rural lodges may provide internet access, the service can be slower or less reliable due to the remoteness of the location. In these areas, it's a good idea to have an alternative form of communication, such as mobile data, especially if you'll be using navigation apps or need to stay in touch with others during your trip.

When it comes to mobile communication in Iceland, the country has excellent mobile coverage across most regions. There are three main mobile service providers in Iceland: Síminn, Vodafone, and Nova. These companies provide coverage throughout the country, including urban areas and many rural regions. However, it's important to note that while coverage is good in most inhabited parts of Iceland, there are some remote areas, particularly in the highlands and certain sections of the Westfjords, where mobile signals can be weak or non-existent. If you're planning on hiking or traveling in these more isolated areas, it's a good idea to be aware of the potential for limited mobile service and to plan accordingly by informing others of your route or carrying a portable satellite communication device for emergencies.

For tourists, one of the most convenient ways to stay connected during their trip to Iceland is by purchasing a local SIM card. SIM cards from Icelandic providers are widely available and can be purchased at the airport upon arrival, in convenience stores, or at mobile phone shops in Reykjavík and other towns. Purchasing a prepaid SIM card is an affordable and practical option if you want to use mobile data during your stay without relying solely on Wi-Fi. The SIM cards usually come with a set amount of data, and you can choose a plan that best fits your needs, depending on how much internet usage you expect during your trip.

For example, Síminn and Vodafone both offer tourist SIM cards that include a combination of data, minutes, and text messages. These SIM cards are typically valid for a certain number of days and can be recharged if you need more data during your stay. By using a local SIM card, you can avoid expensive international roaming charges from your home provider and still have access to high-speed 4G or even 5G networks in most parts of the country. Installing a local SIM card is simple: you just insert it into your phone and follow the setup instructions provided by the carrier.

If you're traveling from Europe, you may be able to use your current mobile phone plan in Iceland without incurring extra charges, thanks to the European Union's roaming agreements. Iceland, while not an EU member, is part of the European Economic Area (EEA), which means that citizens of EU and EEA countries can often use their mobile plans in Iceland without paying additional fees for roaming. However, it's always a good idea to check with your mobile provider before your trip to confirm whether your plan includes free or reduced-rate roaming in Iceland. For travelers from outside Europe, such as those from the United States or Canada, it's generally more cost-effective to purchase a local SIM card rather than use international roaming, which can quickly become expensive.

For those who prefer not to switch SIM cards, another option is to use an international roaming package provided by your home carrier. Many mobile providers offer international plans that allow you to use your phone abroad for a set daily or weekly fee. These plans typically include data, calls, and text messages, although the rates can vary depending on the provider. If you don't plan on using a lot of mobile data during your trip and will primarily rely on Wi-Fi, an international roaming plan might be a good alternative. However, keep in mind that these packages can still be more expensive than using a local SIM card, especially if you're planning an extended stay in Iceland.

In addition to mobile data, another option for staying connected while traveling in Iceland is renting a portable Wi-Fi device, also known as a mobile hotspot. These devices allow you to create your own personal Wi-Fi network wherever you go, using Iceland's mobile data network to connect to the internet. Portable Wi-Fi devices are available for rent at Keflavík International Airport, in Reykjavík, and through various online services. They are particularly useful for travelers who need to connect multiple devices, such as phones, tablets, and laptops, without purchasing separate SIM cards for each device. Portable Wi-Fi devices usually come with a data allowance, and once you reach your data limit, you can either purchase additional data or continue using the device at reduced speeds.

For tourists who are staying in Iceland for an extended period or who need consistent access to the internet for work, renting a portable Wi-Fi device can be a great solution, especially in areas where public Wi-Fi might not be available.

It's important to book these devices in advance, as availability can be limited, especially during the peak tourist season.

Communication in Iceland also extends beyond internet access and mobile data. Iceland is known for having an efficient and modern postal service, and if you want to send postcards or packages home, the Icelandic postal service, Íslandspóstur, operates throughout the country. Post offices are easy to find in Reykjavík and other towns, and many tourist shops and hotels sell postcards and stamps. Sending a postcard from Iceland is a nice way to share your travels with loved ones back home, and the postal service is generally reliable.

If you need to make international calls during your trip to Iceland, the most cost-effective method is usually to use internet-based communication apps like WhatsApp, Skype, or FaceTime, which allow you to make voice or video calls over Wi-Fi or mobile data. These apps are free to use, aside from data charges, and are widely available on smartphones and computers. Given the widespread availability of high-speed internet in Iceland, using these apps is often the easiest way to stay in touch with family and friends without incurring high international calling charges.

Iceland offers excellent internet and communication services for tourists, making it easy to stay connected during your trip. With high-speed internet available in most parts of the country, mobile coverage extending to even remote areas, and a variety of affordable options for SIM cards and data plans, travelers can access the communication tools they need while exploring Iceland's stunning landscapes. Whether you're relying on Wi-Fi in the city, using mobile data in the countryside, or renting a portable Wi-Fi device for more remote adventures, Iceland's communication infrastructure ensures that you can stay in touch, find your way your way, and share your experiences with ease.

Important Applications and Tools

When traveling to Iceland, there are several important applications and tools that can significantly enhance your experience. These apps and tools can assist with everything from navigating the country's breathtaking landscapes to staying updated on local weather conditions, finding accommodation, and ensuring your safety during your adventures. With Iceland's remote areas, unpredictable weather, and unique natural features, having the right apps can help make your trip smoother, more enjoyable, and stress-free.

One of the most important types of apps you'll need in Iceland is a reliable navigation tool. Iceland's landscapes are vast, and many tourists travel by rental car or bus to look around different parts of the island. Google Maps is widely used and works well in Iceland for general navigation. It can help you find your way through cities and towns, as well as rural roads and popular tourist sites. Google Maps provides information on distances, estimated travel times, and directions, which is particularly useful if you're unfamiliar with the area. However, one thing to keep in mind is that Google Maps may not always be accurate for certain remote or unpaved roads, especially in more isolated parts of the country.

In addition to Google Maps, Maps.me is another useful navigation tool that allows you to download offline maps of Iceland. This app can be invaluable if you're traveling to areas where internet access or mobile signal might be weak or nonexistent. Maps.me uses GPS to help you find your way without relying on mobile data, which makes it an excellent tool for hiking, driving, or exploring remote parts of Iceland. You can download specific maps of regions or trails ahead of time, ensuring that you can find your way even if you lose signal during your trip.

Another essential tool for tourists in Iceland is a weather app. Iceland's weather is famously unpredictable, with conditions changing rapidly throughout the day. It's not uncommon to experience sunshine, rain, and snow all within a few hours, even in the summer. Having an accurate and up-to-date weather app will allow you to stay informed about current conditions and help you plan your day accordingly. The Icelandic Met Office (Veðurstofa Íslands) offers a weather app that provides real-time updates on temperature, wind speed, precipitation, and other important weather factors. This app is particularly useful for hikers, drivers, and anyone engaging in outdoor activities, as it includes warnings about potential weather hazards like storms, heavy winds, or icy roads.

Another weather app that's widely used in Iceland is Yr.no, which is operated by the Norwegian Meteorological Institute. While it's not Iceland-specific, it's considered to be one of the most accurate weather forecasting tools for the region. The app provides detailed weather forecasts and can give you a clear idea of what to expect over the next few days. Given the nature of Iceland's weather, checking the forecast regularly can help you avoid being caught off guard by sudden changes in conditions.

For those planning to travel during the winter or visit remote areas, having access to information on road conditions is also crucial. Iceland has a dedicated app called SafeTravel, which provides information on road closures, driving conditions, and travel warnings. SafeTravel is designed with tourists in mind and is run by the Icelandic Association for Search and Rescue (ICE-SAR). The app includes updates on road safety, advice on how to stay safe in various weather conditions, and even a feature that allows you to register your travel plans in case you are venturing into more dangerous or isolated areas. By using this app, you can receive notifications about any potential hazards on your route, helping you make informed decisions about whether to proceed or adjust your plans.

Another key app for travelers, especially those interested in experiencing Iceland's natural beauty, is the Aurora Forecast app. One of the main attractions for visitors to Iceland during the winter months is the chance to see the Northern Lights, also known as the Aurora Borealis. The Aurora Forecast app provides detailed predictions on the likelihood of seeing the Northern Lights, including information on solar activity and cloud cover, which are crucial for determining visibility. The app offers forecasts for specific locations and helps you decide where and when to go for the best chance of witnessing this stunning natural phenomenon. The app's real-time alerts are particularly useful, as they notify you when conditions are favorable for spotting the Northern Lights.

For accommodation, booking, and food, apps like Booking.com and Airbnb are very popular in Iceland. They allow tourists to search for and book accommodations ranging from hotels and guesthouses to cabins and apartments. Iceland has a wide variety of lodging options, and these apps make it easy to compare prices, read reviews, and secure your stay in advance. Many tourists choose to book their accommodations through these platforms because they offer flexibility in terms of price and availability, especially during the busy tourist season. Booking.com, for instance, offers a range of options for different budgets, while Airbnb allows travelers to find more unique and personalized accommodations, such as farm stays or vacation homes.

In addition to accommodation, apps like Yelp and TripAdvisor can help you find the best restaurants and dining experiences in Iceland. Reykjavík, in particular, has a thriving food scene, with everything from traditional Icelandic cuisine to international dishes available. These apps allow you to browse through reviews and ratings from other travelers, making it easier to choose the right restaurant or café. Whether you're looking for local seafood, vegetarian options, or a cozy café to relax in, these apps can guide you to the best spots based on your preferences.

For those who want to look around Iceland's hiking trails and natural sites, the AllTrails app is a valuable resource. AllTrails provides detailed information on hiking routes, including difficulty levels, trail lengths, elevation changes, and user reviews. The app is particularly useful for tourists who want to look around Iceland's vast wilderness on foot, as it includes information on well-known trails as well as lesser-known paths. Whether you're planning to hike in Þingvellir National Park, the Laugavegur Trail, or the highlands, AllTrails offers detailed maps and user tips that can help you prepare for the trip. Similar to Maps.me, AllTrails also offers the option to download maps for offline use, which is important in areas where there may be no mobile signal.

Another useful tool for communication in Iceland is WhatsApp or similar messaging apps like Facebook Messenger or Skype. Given Iceland's excellent internet infrastructure, many tourists and locals alike rely on these apps for communication rather than traditional phone calls or SMS messages. If you're traveling with family or friends, using a messaging app allows you to stay in touch while avoiding international calling fees. These apps also support video calls and group chats, making it easy to coordinate plans or check in with loved ones back home.

For tourists who are planning to drive in Iceland, having a fuel app like GasBuddy or the N1 app can be useful for finding the nearest gas stations and checking fuel prices. While gas stations are readily available in larger towns and along the Ring Road, they can be more spread out in remote areas. The N1 app is particularly handy because it shows the locations of N1 gas stations, which are common throughout the country, and offers information on their services, such as food, restrooms, and car maintenance options. Using these apps ensures that you can plan your fuel stops in advance, especially when traveling to more isolated regions where gas stations may be few and far between.

Lastly, it's important to have a currency converter app to help you manage your budget while in Iceland. The official currency in Iceland is the Icelandic króna (ISK), and using a currency converter app allows you to quickly and easily calculate the cost of goods and services in your home currency. Apps like XE Currency or Currency Converter are popular choices that offer real-time exchange rates and allow you to convert amounts without needing to connect to the internet. This can be particularly useful when shopping, dining out, or booking tours, helping you stay on top of your expenses.

CHAPTER 4

LOCAL KNOWLEDGE FOR A SMOOTH TRIP

Local Etiquette, Customs, Laws and Taboos

Understanding local etiquette, customs, laws, and taboos is essential for any tourist visiting Iceland, as it helps ensure a respectful and enjoyable experience both for travelers and the local population. Iceland has its own unique cultural traditions, legal framework, and social norms, which, while often aligned with other Scandinavian countries, carry distinct features that may be unfamiliar to visitors.

Icelanders are generally known for their friendliness, politeness, and laid-back approach to life. However, this doesn't mean that Iceland is devoid of social expectations. For instance, one of the most fundamental elements of Icelandic etiquette is the value placed on personal space and privacy. Iceland has a small population, and as a result, locals are accustomed to respecting each other's boundaries, both physically and emotionally. In public settings, such as restaurants, cafes, or public transportation, it's important to maintain a respectful distance and avoid being overly intrusive or loud. Icelanders tend to be reserved in public, and while they are friendly and open to conversations with tourists, they usually prefer to avoid unnecessary attention.

As a tourist, it's polite to mirror this behavior and be considerate of personal space.

When greeting someone in Iceland, a simple handshake is the most common form of introduction, especially in formal settings or when meeting someone for the first time. Icelanders often use their first names, even in formal or professional contexts, as there are no family names in Icelandic tradition. Instead, people use a patronymic or matronymic system, meaning that their last name reflects their parent's first name followed by either "son" or "dóttir" (son or daughter). For example, if a person's father is named Jón, their last name would be Jónsson or Jónsdóttir. This is important to keep in mind when addressing people, as using first names is the norm, even when speaking to someone in an official capacity.

Punctuality is another important aspect of Icelandic culture. Whether it's for a meeting, a tour, or even a casual coffee date, being on time is considered a sign of respect. Icelanders value their time and expect others to do the same, so it's a good idea to make sure you arrive promptly for any scheduled events. If you're going to be late, it's polite to inform the person or group you're meeting with as soon as possible, as this demonstrates that you value their time.

When it comes to tipping, Iceland does not have a strong tipping culture. In restaurants, bars, taxis, and other service industries, tipping is neither expected nor required, as service charges are typically included in the final bill. However, if you feel that the service you received was exceptional, leaving a small tip as a gesture of appreciation is acceptable, but it should never be viewed as mandatory. Icelandic workers are paid a fair wage, and the lack of tipping culture reflects the country's strong emphasis on equality and fairness in the workplace.

In terms of customs, one of the most important things to be aware of in Iceland is the deep respect for nature and the environment. Iceland's landscape is one of its most precious assets, and locals take great pride in preserving the country's natural beauty. As a tourist, it's essential to follow the principle of "leave no trace." This means that you should always clean up after yourself, avoid littering, and stay on designated paths when hiking or exploring the countryside. Off-road driving is strictly prohibited in Iceland, as it can cause irreparable damage to the fragile ecosystem, and those caught doing so face heavy fines. Respecting nature is not just an expectation in Iceland but a way of life, and visitors are encouraged to do the same by following the rules and being mindful of their impact on the environment.

Another aspect of Icelandic culture that may be unfamiliar to tourists is the local attitude toward hot springs and public swimming pools, which are an integral part of life in Iceland. Icelanders' frequent geothermal pools for both relaxation and socializing, and there is a specific etiquette associated with visiting these places. Before entering any public pool or hot spring, it is required to shower thoroughly without a swimsuit. This is not just a suggestion, but a strict rule that is taken seriously in Iceland. The purpose of the shower is to ensure that the pools remain clean, as they are not heavily chlorinated like pools in other countries. Visitors who fail to shower properly before entering the pool may be asked to do so by staff or even other patrons. It's important to respect this custom and follow the rules to avoid offending locals or causing discomfort.

In addition to local customs, tourists should also be aware of Iceland's laws, particularly those related to alcohol, smoking, and drugs. Alcohol is only sold in government-regulated stores called Vínbúðin, and you won't find it for sale in regular supermarkets or convenience stores. The legal drinking age in Iceland is 20, and this law is strictly enforced. If you plan to buy alcohol, be prepared to show identification, and note that Vínbúðin stores have limited operating hours, often closing early in the evening and remaining closed on Sundays. Public consumption of alcohol is generally frowned upon, and it's illegal to drink in public spaces, including parks or on the street.

Smoking is also heavily regulated in Iceland. It is illegal to smoke in enclosed public spaces, including restaurants, bars, and public transportation. Additionally, many hotels and guesthouses have strict non-smoking policies, and smoking indoors can result in hefty fines. Icelanders take health and well-being seriously, and smoking rates in the country are relatively low compared to other parts of Europe. If you smoke, be mindful of designated smoking areas, which are usually clearly marked.

One area where Iceland differs significantly from some other countries is its attitude toward drugs. Iceland has very strict drug laws, and the possession, use, or sale of any illegal drugs, including marijuana, is punishable by law. Tourists should be aware that Icelandic authorities do not tolerate drug offenses, and those caught with drugs face serious legal consequences, including potential jail time or heavy fines. It's important to abide by the law and avoid bringing any prohibited substances into the country.

In terms of social taboos, Iceland is a relatively progressive and tolerant society, but there are still some cultural norms that tourists should be mindful of. One such norm is the emphasis on gender equality. Iceland is known for being one of the most gender-equal countries in the world, and sexism or discrimination based on gender is not tolerated in any form. Women in Iceland are highly respected and often hold positions of power in both the public and private sectors. As a tourist, it's important to respect this equality and avoid making gender-based assumptions or comments that could be perceived as disrespectful.

Another important social expectation in Iceland is the value placed on honesty and straightforwardness. Icelanders are known for being direct and honest in their communication, and they generally appreciate the same from others. Being overly formal or indirect can sometimes come across as insincere or evasive. If you need help or have a question, Icelanders are usually happy to assist, but they prefer a straightforward approach. Being polite and respectful is, of course, important, but there's no need to use flowery language or excessive politeness when asking for help.

Religion plays a relatively minor role in everyday life for most Icelanders, but the country has a long history of Christianity, particularly Lutheranism. While Iceland is not a particularly religious society, with many Icelanders identifying as secular or atheist, there are still some churches and religious traditions that are respected. If visiting a church or religious site, it's important to behave respectfully, dress appropriately, and avoid loud or disruptive behavior.

The Language and Key Phrases

Icelandic is the official language of Iceland, and it is deeply tied to the country's culture, history, and national identity. Icelandic has its roots in Old Norse, the language of the Vikings who settled in Iceland more than a thousand years ago. Over time, Icelandic has evolved, but it remains one of the oldest and least-changed languages in the world. For tourists visiting Iceland, understanding the basics of the language and being familiar with a few key phrases can enhance the travel experience. While most Icelanders speak excellent English, especially in cities and tourist areas, learning some Icelandic phrases can help you connect with the local culture and show respect for the country you're visiting.

Icelandic is a Germanic language, closely related to other Scandinavian languages like Faroese and Norwegian, though it has preserved many archaic features that have disappeared from its relatives. One of the most notable aspects of Icelandic is its complex grammar. Icelandic uses four grammatical cases (nominative, accusative, dative, and genitive) and has a system of verb conjugations that can be challenging for those unfamiliar with the language. Additionally, Icelandic nouns have three grammatical genders: masculine, feminine, and neuter, and adjectives and articles must agree with the gender, case, and number of the noun they describe. This can make learning Icelandic somewhat difficult for beginners, but for tourists, there's no need to worry about mastering the intricacies of the language during your visit. A basic understanding of key phrases will go a long way in helping you get by and engage with locals.

One of the first things you'll notice about Icelandic is the length and complexity of some of the words. Icelandic words can be long, as they are often created by combining smaller words into compounds. For example, the Icelandic word for "volcano" is "eldfjall," which literally translates to "fire mountain." The word for "airport" is "flugvöllur," meaning "flight field." While these long compound words can seem intimidating at first, many of them are logical and descriptive, and once you break them down, they are easier to understand.

For tourists, the good news is that most Icelanders are multilingual and have a very high proficiency in English. In fact, English is taught in schools from an early age, and many Icelanders also speak other languages like Danish or German. This means that you'll rarely encounter language barriers when visiting popular tourist destinations, hotels, restaurants, or shops. That being said, Icelanders greatly appreciate when visitors make an effort to learn a few words or phrases in Icelandic, even if it's just basic greetings or expressions of politeness.

The most common greeting in Icelandic is "Halló," which is used much like "hello" in English. Another friendly and widely used greeting is "Góðan daginn," which means "Good day" and can be used during the daytime. This phrase is slightly more formal than "Halló" but is a polite and common way to greet people. If you're greeting someone in the evening, you can say "Góða kvöldið," meaning "Good evening." These greetings are simple and easy to remember, and using them can help make a good impression when you first meet someone.

When interacting with locals, basic phrases of politeness are always useful. Saying "Takk" or "Takk fyrir" means "Thank you" and is a polite way to show gratitude. Icelanders appreciate it when tourists take the time to thank them in their own language, and it's a small gesture that can go a long way. If you want to say "You're welcome," you can say "Verði þér að góðu," although in casual conversation, it's common to simply reply with "Ekkert mál," which means "No problem." Learning these simple phrases can help you find your way everyday interactions with ease.

If you need to apologize or excuse yourself, the phrase "Fyrirgefðu" is the Icelandic equivalent of "Excuse me" or "I'm sorry." This can be used in a variety of situations, whether you're trying to get someone's attention, accidentally bump into someone, or need to apologize for a minor mistake. Another useful phrase is "Afsakið," which also means "Excuse me" and can be used when trying to politely get through a crowd or ask for directions.

When asking for help or information, knowing how to ask basic questions can be helpful. The word for "Where" in Icelandic is "Hvar," so if you need to ask where something is, you can use it in a simple question like "Hvar er…" followed by the place or thing you're looking for. For example, "Hvar er salerni?" means "Where is the bathroom?" and "Hvar er hótelið?" means "Where is the hotel?" Another common phrase is "Hvað kostar þetta?" which means "How much does this cost?" and can be useful when shopping or dining out.

While Icelanders are known for their excellent English skills, there may be times when you encounter someone who speaks limited English, particularly in more rural areas. In such cases, knowing how to ask if someone speaks English can be very helpful. The phrase "Talarðu ensku?" means "Do you speak English?" and is a polite way to inquire if someone is comfortable communicating in English. If you're unsure about how to pronounce a word or phrase, don't be afraid to ask for help. Icelanders are generally patient and understanding when it comes to foreigners attempting to speak their language, and they're often happy to assist with pronunciation or offer an English translation.

One of the challenges of learning Icelandic is its pronunciation, which can be quite different from English. The Icelandic alphabet includes several letters that do not exist in English, such as "þ" (thorn) and "ð" (eth). The letter "þ" is pronounced like the "th" in the English word "think," while "ð" is pronounced like the "th" in "that." Additionally, Icelandic has a number of vowels sounds that can be difficult for non-native speakers to master. For tourists, however, it's not necessary to perfect these sounds. Most Icelanders will understand what you're trying to say, even if your pronunciation isn't perfect.

In terms of signage, most public signs in Iceland, including those at tourist attractions, airports, and public transportation, are written in both Icelandic and English, making it easy for tourists to find your way without needing to rely solely on Icelandic. However, if you're venturing into more rural or off-the-beaten-path areas, you may encounter fewer English translations, so having a basic understanding of Icelandic words and phrases can be helpful in these situations.

Another important aspect of the Icelandic language is its connection to Icelandic culture and literature. Icelanders are extremely proud of their literary heritage, which dates back to the medieval sagas. These sagas, written in Old Norse, are still widely read and studied in Iceland today, and they form a key part of the country's national identity. For many Icelanders, preserving the Icelandic language is a way of maintaining a direct link to their history and cultural traditions. As a tourist, learning even a few words of Icelandic can help you gain a deeper appreciation of this rich cultural history.

In addition to greetings and polite expressions, it's useful to know some basic Icelandic phrases related to food and dining, especially if you plan to look around local restaurants or markets. The word for "food" is "matur," and if you want to ask for the menu, you can say "Get ég fengið matseðilinn?"

which means "Can I have the menu?" If you have dietary restrictions or preferences, you can use phrases like "Ég er grænmetisæta," meaning "I am a vegetarian," or "Ég er með ofnæmi fyrir..." followed by the food you're allergic to. For example, "Ég er með ofnæmi fyrir hnetum" means "I am allergic to nuts." Knowing these phrases can make dining out in Iceland easier and ensure that you can communicate your needs clearly to restaurant staff.

Finally, Icelandic has a strong sense of community, and locals value politeness, friendliness, and respect for others. As a tourist, using even a few Icelandic phrases will not only help you find your way daily interactions but will also show that you appreciate the local culture and are making an effort to engage with it. Icelanders are generally very welcoming to tourists, and they'll often be pleased when visitors try to speak their language, even if it's just a simple "Takk" or "Góðan daginn."

Local Language Learning Resources

When traveling to Iceland, one of the ways tourists can deepen their connection with the country is by engaging with the Icelandic language. Though English is widely spoken, learning some Icelandic can offer a richer, more immersive experience. For those interested in picking up Icelandic, there are a number of resources, both local and online, that can make the process accessible and rewarding. These resources are designed to accommodate different learning levels, from beginners to more advanced speakers.

Icelandic is unique because of its historical roots in Old Norse, the language spoken by the Vikings. This connection makes Icelandic not only a tool for communication but also a gateway to understanding the country's history, literature, and culture. While learning Icelandic might seem challenging at first due to its grammar, vocabulary, and pronunciation, the tools and resources available today make it possible to learn in a way that is engaging and manageable for tourists. By using these resources, visitors can start to familiarize themselves with the language before arriving in Iceland or while they are exploring the country.

For tourists who are in Iceland and want to immerse themselves in the language, one of the most accessible resources is interacting with locals. Icelanders are generally friendly and patient when it comes to language learners, and many appreciate when tourists make an effort to speak a few words in Icelandic, even if their pronunciation isn't perfect. Simple greetings like "Góðan daginn" (Good day) or "Takk fyrir" (Thank you) can go a long way in showing respect for the local culture. Icelanders are usually happy to help tourists with pronunciation or explain the meaning of words if asked politely. Engaging in short conversations with locals can be one of the best ways to practice and gain confidence in speaking the language.

For those who prefer a more structured approach, there are several Icelandic language schools and courses available in Reykjavík and other major towns. These courses range from beginner-level classes to more advanced language instruction. One notable option is the Icelandic Language

School (Íslenska fyrir alla), which offers courses designed specifically for foreigners who want to learn Icelandic. These classes typically focus on conversational skills, vocabulary building, and basic grammar, making them ideal for tourists or short-term visitors who want to pick up practical language skills that can be used in everyday interactions. Classes are usually offered in group settings, and many schools have flexible schedules to accommodate the needs of tourists who may only be staying in Iceland for a short time.

Another useful resource for learning Icelandic is the Icelandic Online language learning platform. This is a free, web-based program that is available to anyone interested in learning the language, whether they are in Iceland or abroad. The program is developed by the University of Iceland and offers courses that range from beginner to advanced levels. Icelandic Online is particularly useful because it allows learners to progress at their own pace and provides interactive exercises that focus on reading, writing, listening, and speaking skills. The platform includes audio recordings of native speakers, which can help with pronunciation and listening comprehension. For tourists who are looking for a flexible and free option to learn Icelandic, Icelandic Online is a valuable tool that can be accessed from anywhere.

For tourists already in Iceland, libraries can also be a great resource for learning the language. Many libraries in Reykjavík and other towns offer Icelandic language learning materials, including books, dictionaries, and audio resources that can help tourists practice their skills. In addition, some libraries offer language exchange programs, where tourists can meet Icelanders who are interested in learning English or other languages in exchange for helping the tourist practice Icelandic. These language exchange programs can be an enjoyable and informal way to improve conversational skills while meeting locals.

Additionally, there are several mobile apps available that can help tourists learn Icelandic in a convenient and engaging way. Apps like Duolingo, Memrise, and Babbel all offer Icelandic language courses that are specifically designed for beginners. These apps use a gamified approach to language learning, with short lessons that focus on vocabulary, sentence structure, and pronunciation. One of the advantages of using a mobile app is that it allows tourists to practice Icelandic in their spare time, whether they're waiting for a bus, relaxing in a café, or traveling between destinations. Many of these apps also track progress and adjust the lessons based on the learner's proficiency, making it easier to build language skills incrementally.

Another excellent resource for tourists is the Icelandic language learning podcasts and YouTube channels available online. Podcasts like "Icelandic for Foreigners" provide lessons on vocabulary, grammar, and cultural context, making them an easy way to learn the language while on the go. Similarly, YouTube channels focused on teaching Icelandic often provide visual lessons, which can be especially helpful for understanding pronunciation and sentence structure. For tourists who enjoy multimedia learning, these podcasts and videos offer an engaging way to supplement more formal language study or casual practice.

For tourists with a particular interest in Icelandic literature, reading books written in Icelandic or translated into Icelandic can be a fun and immersive way to engage with the language. Although Icelandic literature can be challenging for beginners, starting with simple texts like children's books or bilingual books can help build vocabulary and comprehension skills. Many bookstores in Reykjavík, such as Eymundsson, offer a selection of Icelandic books with English translations, which can serve as a helpful bridge for learners who want to challenge themselves while still having access to an English reference. Reading Icelandic newspapers, magazines, or even simple brochures can also help learners pick up new words and phrases that are relevant to daily life in Iceland.

For tourists who are more interested in learning conversational Icelandic, audio learning tools such as Pimsleur's Icelandic or Teach Yourself Icelandic can be excellent options. These audio courses are designed to focus on speaking and listening skills, which are particularly useful for travelers who want to communicate in real-life situations. These programs emphasize repetition and gradual vocabulary building, helping learners internalize common phrases and develop better pronunciation over time. Since they are audio-based, tourists can listen to these lessons while traveling, hiking, or even relaxing, making them a flexible option for those on the move.

Cultural immersion can also serve as a language learning resource for tourists. By participating in local cultural events, festivals, or social gatherings, tourists can expose themselves to the Icelandic language in a natural context. Even if you don't understand everything being said, listening to the language in conversation can improve your familiarity with its sounds and rhythms. Many cultural events in Iceland, such as concerts, theater performances, or public lectures, may be held in Icelandic, and attending these events can give tourists a deeper sense of how the language is used in everyday life.

For tourists who plan to spend an extended period of time in Iceland, private language tutors are another resource worth considering. There are several language tutors in Reykjavík and other cities who offer private lessons tailored to the individual needs of the learner. While private lessons can be more expensive than group classes, they provide personalized instruction and allow tourists to focus on specific areas of difficulty, whether that's pronunciation, grammar, or conversation. Private tutors can also offer cultural insights alongside language instruction, giving learners a more holistic understanding of Icelandic society.

Finally, Icelandic cultural centers and museums can also serve as language learning resources for tourists. Many cultural centers, such as the Nordic House in Reykjavík, host events, exhibitions, and workshops that focus on Icelandic language and culture. These institutions often provide materials and resources that help visitors engage with the Icelandic language in a cultural context. Whether it's through a guided tour in Icelandic, a language-focused exhibition, or a workshop on Icelandic literature, these cultural centers offer tourists opportunities to learn the language in a more immersive and interactive way.

CHAPTER 5

STAYING SAFE AND HEALTHY

Health Care and Safety

When traveling to Iceland, it is essential to understand the healthcare system and the safety measures that can ensure a safe and enjoyable trip. Iceland is known for being one of the safest countries in the world, with a highly developed healthcare system that tourists can access if needed. Whether you're planning to look around the country's cities, hike through its wilderness, or simply relax in a geothermal pool, knowing how to handle health and safety issues can give you peace of mind.

Iceland's healthcare system is public and operates under the Ministry of Health. It is known for being efficient and well-organized, with modern medical facilities and highly trained professionals. For Icelandic citizens and residents, healthcare is funded by the government, but tourists will need to pay for any medical services they receive unless they are covered by travel insurance or are citizens of countries that have reciprocal healthcare agreements with Iceland. For example, citizens of the European Economic Area (EEA) who carry a European Health Insurance Card (EHIC) can access necessary medical treatment at the same cost as Icelanders, though this card does not cover everything, such as private healthcare or non-essential treatments. For visitors from countries outside the EEA, it's highly recommended to have comprehensive travel insurance that covers medical expenses.

In case you need medical assistance while in Iceland, the country's healthcare system is very accessible, especially in larger towns and cities like Reykjavík and Akureyri. Reykjavík, the capital, is home to Landspítali University Hospital, the largest hospital in Iceland, which provides a wide range of medical services, including emergency care. There are also several smaller health clinics and private medical facilities throughout the city. If you find yourself in a medical emergency, you can call 112, which is Iceland's emergency number for ambulance services, police, and fire departments. The emergency response time in urban areas is generally quick, and the standard of care is high.

Outside of Reykjavík, healthcare facilities are more limited, but most towns have health clinics, known as "heilsugæsla," where you can receive basic medical care. These clinics typically offer services such as general practitioner consultations, minor treatments, and prescriptions. In more rural or remote areas, access to medical care can be more challenging, so it's important to be prepared, especially if you are planning activities like hiking in the highlands or exploring remote parts of the Westfjords. In these cases, having travel insurance that includes emergency evacuation coverage is especially important, as rescue operations in Iceland can be expensive and logistically difficult due to the country's rugged terrain.

Pharmacies in Iceland, known as "apótek," are well-stocked with over-the-counter medications, and most pharmacists speak English, making it easy for tourists to get advice or purchase basic medications for minor ailments like headaches, colds, or allergies. Prescription medications are also available, but you will need a prescription from a doctor to obtain them. Pharmacies are typically open during regular business hours, though in Reykjavík, you can find some that stay open later or even operate 24 hours a day. If you take regular medication, it's advisable to bring enough for the duration of your stay, along with a copy of your prescription in case you need a refill during your trip.

For tourists visiting Iceland, it's important to be aware of the country's unique natural environment and the potential health and safety risks associated with outdoor activities. Iceland's landscape is stunning but can also be dangerous if proper precautions aren't taken. The weather, in particular, can change rapidly, and tourists often underestimate the risks posed by the cold, wind, and rain. Hypothermia is a real danger, even in the summer months, especially for those hiking or engaging in outdoor activities in remote areas. Dressing in layers and wearing weather-appropriate clothing, such as waterproof and windproof outer layers, is essential for staying warm and dry. It's also important to check the weather forecast regularly, particularly if you are planning to spend time outdoors, as conditions can shift quickly and dramatically.

Hiking is a popular activity in Iceland, but it's crucial to be well-prepared before setting off on a hike, especially in remote or less-traveled areas. Many trails are not as clearly marked as those in other countries, and some lead through rough or dangerous terrain. Always tell someone your planned route and estimated return time, whether it's the staff at your accommodation or a friend or family member. The SafeTravel app, developed by the Icelandic Association for Search and Rescue, allows you to submit your travel plans, and in the event of an emergency, rescue teams can use this information to locate you more quickly.

River crossings are common on many hiking trails, especially in the highlands, and can be hazardous due to fast-moving water or unpredictable depth. Never attempt to cross a river without first assessing its safety, and if in doubt, turn back or find another route. Similarly, Iceland's glaciers and volcanic landscapes can be dangerous for those unfamiliar with these environments. If you plan to hike on a glacier, it's essential to go with a licensed guide, as glaciers have hidden crevasses and other risks that can be fatal if not properly find your wayd.

In addition to hiking, many tourists visit Iceland for its geothermal hot springs, which are scattered across the country. While these hot springs are one of Iceland's most famous attractions, they can pose safety risks if not approached correctly. Some hot springs, especially those in more remote areas, can be scalding hot or contain dangerous chemicals. It's crucial to stick to well-known, marked springs and avoid entering any water that does not have clear signage indicating it is safe. Always check the temperature of the water before getting in, as even in well-known springs, temperatures can fluctuate.

Another common safety issue in Iceland relates to road travel. Iceland's roads are generally well-maintained, but driving in Iceland presents its own set of challenges, particularly for tourists who may not be used to the country's conditions. Many roads in rural areas, especially those leading to popular tourist sites like waterfalls, mountains, or beaches, are gravel roads that can be slippery or rough. Driving on these roads requires caution and slower speeds, especially if you're unfamiliar with driving on gravel. In the winter, roads can be icy or snow-covered, making driving even more hazardous. It's important to rent a car that is appropriate for the conditions, such as a 4x4 if you plan to drive on F-roads, which are mountain roads that often require river crossings and are only open in the summer. Before setting out on a long drive, check the Icelandic Road and Coastal Administration website or app for updates on road conditions and closures.

Seatbelt use is mandatory in Iceland, and fines for not wearing one are strictly enforced. Icelandic law also prohibits using mobile phones while driving unless you use a hands-free device. Additionally, Iceland has very strict drunk driving laws, with a zero-tolerance policy. Even a small amount of alcohol in your system can result in hefty fines or even jail time, so it's important to avoid drinking if you plan to drive.

Iceland's tap water is among the cleanest and safest in the world, and there's no need to buy bottled water during your stay. The country's water comes directly from natural springs and is free of contaminants. It's safe to drink from the tap in any part of the country, whether you're in a city or a remote area, and many locals will encourage you to avoid buying bottled water as a way to reduce plastic waste. Just remember that hot water in Iceland, which is geothermally heated, often has a sulfuric smell due to the natural minerals present in the water, but it is perfectly safe for bathing or washing.

In terms of general safety, Iceland is known for being a low-crime country. Violent crime is extremely rare, and petty crimes like pickpocketing are also uncommon, even in Reykjavík. That being said, tourists should still practice basic safety measures, such as keeping an eye on personal belongings and avoiding leaving valuables unattended in public places. Icelanders are known for their trustworthiness, and it's not unusual to see locals leaving their doors unlocked or bicycles unattended. However, it's always wise to use common sense and stay vigilant, particularly in crowded tourist areas where petty theft may occur on rare occasions.

Another important health and safety consideration for tourists in Iceland is sun protection. While Iceland's cool climate may not seem like a place where you'd need sunscreen, the country's northern latitude means that UV rays can be stronger than expected, especially during the summer months when daylight lasts for nearly 24 hours. The sun's rays can be particularly intense when reflected off glaciers or snow, so it's important to wear sunscreen, sunglasses, and a hat to protect your skin and eyes when spending time outdoors.

When traveling to a foreign country, it's important to be aware of the emergency contacts and numbers that can provide assistance in case of unforeseen situations. In Iceland, although the country is known for its safety and low crime rates, emergencies can still arise, particularly given the unique natural environment and the potential risks involved in activities such as hiking, driving, or exploring remote areas. Knowing the right emergency numbers and contacts, and understanding how to reach them, can be essential for ensuring a safe and well-prepared trip.

The main emergency number in Iceland is 112, which is used for all emergencies, whether they require police, fire services, an ambulance, or search and rescue. It's important to note that 112 operates 24 hours a day, seven days a week, and is free of charge. The number works anywhere in Iceland, whether you're in the capital city of Reykjavík or in the most remote parts of the countryside. When you dial 112, the operator will determine the nature of your emergency and direct your call to the appropriate response service. Operators are trained to handle calls in Icelandic and English, and they can often assist in other languages as well, making it accessible for tourists.

For health-related emergencies, 112 will connect you to ambulance services or direct you to the nearest medical facility, depending on the severity of the situation. If you or someone you are with experiences a serious medical issue, such as difficulty breathing, a heart attack, or an injury, calling 112 is the fastest way to get help. Ambulances in Iceland are well-equipped, and medical professionals are trained to provide high-quality care en route to the hospital.

If the emergency is related to fire, such as a house fire, wildfire, or any situation where there is a risk of danger from fire, 112 will connect you to the fire department. Firefighters in Iceland are highly skilled and capable of handling both urban fires and rural emergencies, such as forest or grassland fires that may occur during the warmer months. It's important to be aware that Iceland's dry grasslands and strong winds can sometimes cause fires to spread quickly, so tourists should be cautious when camping or using open flames in nature.

For situations involving the police, such as theft, assault, or accidents, dialing 112 will connect you to law enforcement services. While Iceland has one of the lowest crime rates in the world, crimes such as petty theft or car break-ins can still occur, especially in busy tourist areas. If you are a victim of crime or witness one, contacting the police through 112 is the best course of action. Additionally, the police can assist in non-criminal situations, such as lost passports or other travel documents.

Iceland's emergency number 112 also plays a key role in search and rescue operations, which are particularly important given the country's rugged terrain and unpredictable weather conditions. Every year, tourists visit Iceland's beautiful but sometimes dangerous natural attractions, such as glaciers, volcanoes, and waterfalls. These areas, while stunning, can pose risks, especially for those unfamiliar with the landscape or unprepared for sudden changes in weather. If you are lost or injured while hiking, exploring remote areas, or engaging in outdoor activities, dialing 112 can activate Iceland's search and rescue teams, which are composed of highly trained volunteers who specialize in finding and assisting individuals in difficult-to-reach locations. The Icelandic Association for Search and Rescue (ICE-SAR) is renowned for its effectiveness in these operations, and it's crucial to call for help early if you encounter any problems.

In addition to the emergency number 112, there are other important contacts and resources that tourists should be aware of during their stay in Iceland. For medical assistance that is not life-threatening but still requires urgent attention, you can contact the nearest health clinic or hospital. In Reykjavík, the main hospital is Landspítali University Hospital, which is the largest healthcare facility in Iceland. The hospital's emergency room is open 24/7, and it's where you should go if you need urgent medical care but do not require an ambulance. You can also call the hospital directly at 543 1000 to ask for advice or information on medical services.

For non-emergency medical situations, such as minor injuries, illnesses, or needing to refill a prescription, health clinics (heilsugæsla) are available in towns and cities throughout Iceland. Most health clinics operate during regular business hours, but some offer extended or emergency hours, especially in larger towns. Pharmacies (apótek) also serve as a resource for tourists needing over-the-counter medications or medical advice. Pharmacists in Iceland are highly trained, and many speak English, making it easy for tourists to seek advice or obtain basic medications without needing to visit a doctor.

If you find yourself needing to contact your embassy or consulate during your trip to Iceland, it's important to have those numbers handy. Embassies can provide assistance with lost or stolen passports, legal issues, or emergency evacuation in extreme situations. For example, the U.S. Embassy in Reykjavík can be reached at 595 2200, while the British Embassy is contactable at 550 5100. Tourists from other countries should look up their respective embassy or consulate contact details before traveling, as having this information available can save valuable time if issues arise.

For road emergencies, such as vehicle breakdowns or accidents, Iceland has a dedicated road assistance service known as FÍB (Félag íslenskra bifreiðaeigenda), which can be reached at 1777. This number is particularly useful for tourists who are renting cars and traveling outside of the main cities, as rural roads in Iceland can be challenging to find your way, especially in winter. FÍB can assist with flat tires, towing, and other car-related issues. Additionally, the Icelandic Road and Coastal Administration (Vegagerðin) provides information on road conditions and closures, which is vital for those planning to drive in remote areas or during winter. The Road Administration's hotline, 1777, can provide real-time updates on weather-related road closures, hazardous conditions, and other driving risks.

For tourists who are spending time in nature, particularly in areas where weather conditions can change rapidly, the SafeTravel website and app are invaluable resources. SafeTravel provides real-time alerts and warnings about weather, road conditions, and other hazards that may affect tourists. You can register your travel plans on SafeTravel's platform so that authorities know your itinerary in case of an emergency. This is particularly useful for those hiking in remote areas, as it ensures that search and rescue teams have information on your route and expected return time, which can significantly aid in the event of an emergency.

In addition to being aware of emergency contacts and numbers, tourists should take some proactive steps to ensure their safety while traveling in Iceland. First, always check the weather forecast before heading out on any excursions, particularly if you plan to hike, camp, or drive long distances. The Icelandic Met Office provides reliable and up-to-date weather reports, which are essential for planning activities in a country where the weather can shift quickly. Being aware of weather warnings, especially during the winter months, can help prevent accidents or dangerous situations.

Second, if you are renting a car and driving in Iceland, it's important to familiarize yourself with the country's road rules and conditions. The Icelandic Road and Coastal Administration offers a mobile app that provides real-time updates on road conditions, including ice, snow, and closures. Tourists driving in Iceland should also be aware that off-road driving is strictly prohibited, as it can cause significant environmental damage and lead to hefty fines. Sticking to marked roads and following traffic regulations is not only safer but also helps protect Iceland's fragile landscape.

Finally, it's always a good idea to have a basic first aid kit on hand, particularly if you're planning to look around remote areas. While medical assistance in Iceland is generally easy to access in cities and towns, having a few essentials like bandages, antiseptic cream, and pain relievers can be helpful for minor injuries or illnesses. It's also important to carry enough food, water, and warm clothing if you're venturing into rural or wilderness areas, as rescue services can take time to reach remote locations in the event of an emergency.

Travel Scams and How to Avoid Them

When planning a trip to any country, it's important to be aware of potential travel scams and how to avoid falling victim to them. Although Iceland is known for being a safe and relatively crime-free country, as with any tourist destination, there are still occasional reports of scams that target visitors. Tourists may be more vulnerable to scams because they are unfamiliar with the local culture, language, and common practices.

One of the most common scams that can affect tourists in any country, including Iceland, is overcharging, particularly in tourist-heavy areas. Iceland is already known for being an expensive destination, but some businesses may take advantage of visitors by inflating prices or charging hidden fees. This could happen in restaurants, hotels, or taxi services.

For example, tourists may find themselves being charged more than locals for the same service or item. To avoid this, it's important to always check prices before purchasing anything, especially in busy tourist spots. Many restaurants in Iceland post their menus and prices outside their establishments, which allows you to make an informed decision before entering. Additionally, it's a good idea to ask if there are any service charges or additional fees that are not listed on the menu or price list. In taxis, make sure the driver is using a meter or has agreed on a fixed fare before starting the trip.

When it comes to accommodation, booking directly through reputable websites or well-known platforms is the safest way to avoid potential scams. There have been instances where tourists have booked what appeared to be a legitimate accommodation only to arrive and find out that the listing was fake. Scammers may create fraudulent listings on websites or social media, offering attractive deals that are too good to be true, then disappear once the payment has been made. To avoid this, it's crucial to book through trusted platforms like Booking.com or Airbnb, where you can read reviews from other travelers and see verified listings. If a deal seems unusually cheap or suspicious, it's best to steer clear. Always look for properties that have plenty of reviews and high ratings from previous guests.

Another scam that tourists in Iceland should be aware of is the fake tour guide scam. While Iceland is known for its stunning natural beauty and incredible outdoor activities, some unscrupulous individuals may pose as official tour guides without having the necessary qualifications or licenses. These fake guides often offer tours at discounted rates, but they may not have the proper knowledge of the sites or the safety protocols needed for certain activities, such as glacier hiking or exploring caves. In some cases, tourists may be taken to dangerous or restricted areas without their knowledge. To avoid this scam, always book tours through reputable tour companies that have a proven track record. Iceland has many well-established tour operators that are licensed and insured, and they are experts in offering safe and informative experiences. Checking online reviews and asking for recommendations from trusted sources can help ensure that you choose a legitimate and reliable guide.

Currency exchange scams are another potential issue that can affect tourists, particularly those who are not familiar with Iceland's currency, the Icelandic króna (ISK). While this scam is not as prevalent in Iceland as it is in some other countries, it's still important to be cautious when exchanging money. Some exchange services may offer poor rates or charge excessive fees, taking advantage of tourists who may not be aware of the fair exchange rate. To avoid this, it's advisable to exchange currency at banks or official exchange offices rather than using small kiosks or airport services, which may have less favorable rates. Better yet, many tourists find that they don't need to exchange much cash at all in Iceland, as the country is highly cashless, and most businesses accept credit or debit cards, even for small purchases. If you do need to withdraw cash, using an ATM is generally a safer and more cost-effective option than exchanging money at a booth.

Another common scam that can occur in Iceland, as in other tourist destinations, involves rental cars. Many tourists choose to rent a car in Iceland to look around the country's beautiful landscapes at their own pace, but there are some risks associated with this. In some cases, unscrupulous car rental companies may charge tourists for damage that they didn't cause or for pre-existing issues with the vehicle. To avoid this, it's important to thoroughly inspect the car before driving away, taking pictures or videos of any existing damage. Make sure to document even minor scratches or dents, and report them to the rental company immediately so that you are not held responsible later. Additionally, it's a good idea to check the rental company's policy on insurance and any additional fees. Some companies may try to upsell unnecessary insurance or charge for extras that were not clearly outlined in the contract.

Scams related to car rental insurance are another issue that tourists may face. Rental companies may push additional insurance policies that are either overpriced or unnecessary, especially if the traveler already has coverage through their credit card or personal insurance. Before renting a car, it's important to check what is included in your rental agreement and what is covered by your existing insurance. Many credit card companies offer rental car insurance as a benefit, so travelers should verify this before purchasing extra coverage from the rental company. It's also advisable to read the fine print in your rental agreement to avoid being surprised by hidden charges or fees for things like fuel, cleaning, or mileage.

Fake accident scams are less common in Iceland but can happen anywhere tourists are driving. In this type of scam, a local driver may intentionally cause a minor accident or claim that you caused damage to their vehicle in order to extort money from you. They may try to pressure you into paying them directly rather than going through official channels, hoping that you won't want to deal with the hassle of contacting the police or your rental company. If you're involved in any kind of accident, even a minor one, it's essential to report it to the police and your rental car company immediately. Never agree to pay anyone on the spot for damage, and always follow the proper legal procedures.

In addition to these common scams, tourists should be cautious when it comes to online ticketing fraud. Iceland has many popular events and attractions, especially during the summer months when festivals and concerts are frequent. Scammers may create fake websites or advertisements offering discounted tickets to these events, but once the payment is made, the tickets turn out to be invalid or nonexistent. To avoid falling victim to ticketing fraud, always purchase tickets through official event websites or authorized sellers. If a deal seems too good to be true, it likely is. Double-check the legitimacy of the website or seller before making a purchase, and be wary of buying tickets from individuals on social media or online marketplaces.

Credit card fraud is another issue that can affect tourists, though it's relatively rare in Iceland. However, it's still important to be cautious when using your card, especially at ATMs or in unfamiliar locations. To protect yourself from card skimming or fraudulent charges, use ATMs located inside banks or well-lit, secure areas. When paying by card at restaurants, shops, or other establishments, try to keep your card in sight at all times, and don't let it be taken away to another location for processing. It's also a good idea to notify your bank of your travel plans before leaving home to avoid having your card blocked due to unusual activity.

Another common issue that tourists in Iceland might encounter is deceptive advertising or "bait and switch" scams. This occurs when a service or product is advertised at one price or quality level, but when the customer arrives, the actual service or product is significantly different. For example, a tour company might advertise a small group experience, but upon arrival, you find that the group is much larger than promised. Alternatively, a hotel might advertise certain amenities, such as a view or a specific room type, but when you arrive, these features are not available. To avoid falling victim to this type of scam, it's important to research companies and read reviews before booking. Reputable businesses will have a track record of customer satisfaction, and reviews from other travelers can help alert you to any potential red flags.

CHAPTER 6

WHERE TO STAY

When traveling to Iceland, choosing the right accommodation is an important part of planning your trip. Iceland offers a wide range of accommodation options that cater to different types of travelers, from budget-conscious backpackers to those seeking luxury experiences. The type of place you stay will depend on several factors, including your budget, travel style, and the locations you wish to look around. Iceland's tourism infrastructure is well-developed, and there are plenty of options to suit various needs and preferences.

One of the most popular choices for many tourists visiting Iceland is to stay in Reykjavík, the country's capital and largest city. Reykjavík has a variety of accommodation options, ranging from budget hostels to high-end hotels. For travelers looking for a central location with easy access to the city's main attractions, one option is **Hotel Borg**. This historic hotel is situated in the heart of Reykjavík, right across from Austurvöllur Square and near many of the city's most popular sights, such as the Parliament House, Harpa Concert Hall, and the shopping streets of Laugavegur. **Hotel Borg** offers a blend of classic elegance and modern amenities, including free Wi-Fi, a spa, a fitness center, and a restaurant that serves traditional Icelandic dishes. The price range for a stay at **Hotel Borg** typically varies between **$200 to $400 USD per night**, depending on the time of year and the type of room booked. To get to **Hotel Borg** from Keflavík International Airport, which is the main entry point for most international travelers, you can take a shuttle bus, such as the Flybus, or a taxi, which takes around **45 minutes**. You can book directly through the hotel's website or use platforms like **Booking.com** or **Expedia**.

For budget-conscious travelers or backpackers, **Kex Hostel** is a popular choice. Located in a former biscuit factory, **Kex Hostel** is in downtown Reykjavík and provides a unique, industrial-chic atmosphere. This hostel offers both dormitory-style rooms for those traveling on a tight budget and private rooms for guests seeking more privacy. Prices for dormitory beds start at around **$40 USD per night**, while private rooms can cost anywhere from **$100 to $150 USD per night**. **Kex Hostel** features a bar, restaurant, communal kitchen, and a cozy lounge area where guests can relax or meet other travelers. The hostel is also known for hosting live music events, making it a lively and social place to stay. To get to **Kex Hostel** from Keflavík Airport, you can take a shuttle bus or rent a car for the **45-minute drive** to the city center. It's easy to book a stay at **Kex Hostel** through platforms like **Hostelworld, Booking.com**, or the hostel's own website.

If you're a nature lover and prefer to stay outside the city in a more peaceful, scenic setting, **Frost and Fire Hotel** in Hveragerði is a great option. This boutique hotel is located about **40 minutes** east of Reykjavík, in an area known for its geothermal activity and beautiful landscapes. **Frost and Fire Hotel** sits on the banks of the Varmá River and offers breathtaking views of the surrounding mountains and hot springs. The hotel features outdoor hot tubs heated by natural geothermal energy, making it an ideal spot to relax after a day of exploring. Rooms at **Frost and Fire** are modern and cozy, with amenities like free Wi-Fi, flat-screen TVs, and complimentary breakfast. The price range for a stay at **Frost and Fire** is typically between **$150 and $250 USD per night**, depending on the season and room type. Guests can also enjoy the on-site restaurant, which specializes in farm-to-table cuisine made with local ingredients. To get to **Frost and Fire Hotel** from Keflavík Airport, you can rent a car and drive directly, or take a shuttle to Reykjavík and rent a car from there. It's recommended to book directly through the hotel's website or on platforms like **Expedia**.

For travelers seeking a luxurious, once-in-a-lifetime experience, **The Retreat at Blue Lagoon** is one of Iceland's most exclusive accommodations. Located near the famous Blue Lagoon geothermal spa, about **20 minutes** from Keflavík Airport, **The Retreat** offers guests the chance to stay in a luxurious, all-suite hotel with direct access to the Blue Lagoon's mineral-rich waters. The hotel features beautifully designed suites that offer panoramic views of the volcanic landscape, as well as private lagoons where guests can bathe in the warm, healing waters in privacy. Prices for a stay at **The Retreat** start at around **$1,500 USD per night**, making it one of the most expensive accommodations in Iceland, but it offers an unparalleled level of comfort and relaxation. The hotel's amenities include a world-class spa, guided hikes through the surrounding lava fields, and a gourmet restaurant that serves innovative Icelandic cuisine. To get to **The Retreat**, guests can arrange for private airport transfers, or take a shuttle bus to the Blue Lagoon, followed by a short transfer to the hotel. Booking for **The Retreat** can be done through the hotel's official website or luxury travel platforms like **Virtuoso**.

For families or travelers seeking a more rustic, countryside experience, **Hotel Laki** near the town of Kirkjubæjarklaustur in South Iceland is a great choice. This hotel offers a peaceful retreat in the Icelandic countryside, with easy access to natural attractions like the Vatnajökull National Park, Jökulsárlón Glacier Lagoon, and the Fjaðrárgljúfur canyon. **Hotel Laki** has a range of accommodation options, including standard hotel rooms, family rooms, and cottages, making it suitable for families or larger groups. Prices range from **$120 to $200 USD per night**, depending on the type of room or cottage selected. The hotel's amenities include free breakfast, an on-site restaurant serving traditional Icelandic dishes, and outdoor activities like fishing, birdwatching, and hiking. **Hotel Laki** is about a **3-hour drive** from Reykjavík and a **4-hour drive** from Keflavík Airport. Renting a car is the most convenient way to reach **Hotel Laki**, as the area is relatively remote and public transportation options are limited. You can book through the hotel's website or travel platforms like **Booking.com** or **Hotels.com**.

Booking accommodations in Iceland is straightforward, and there are several methods depending on your preferences. Many travelers opt to book through popular online platforms like **Booking.com**, **Expedia**, or **Airbnb**, which offer a wide variety of choices, from hotels to guesthouses to private rentals. These platforms allow you to filter results by price, location, and traveler type, making it easy to find an accommodation that suits your needs. Additionally, booking directly through the hotel's or hostel's website can sometimes offer exclusive deals, discounts, or added perks such as free breakfast or airport transfers.

For travelers looking for last-minute deals or more personalized recommendations, using local travel agencies or booking through Iceland's tourism websites can be helpful. Many local agencies offer package deals that include accommodation, car rentals, and tours, which can simplify the booking process and offer added convenience.

Accessible Travel Tips

Traveling to Iceland can be a remarkable experience, filled with stunning landscapes, vibrant culture, and unique adventures. However, for tourists with disabilities or mobility challenges, navigating this beautiful country requires careful planning and consideration. While Iceland has made strides in improving accessibility in recent years, there are still some challenges to be aware of. By understanding the available resources and planning ahead, travelers can enjoy a fulfilling trip without unnecessary stress.

One of the first steps for accessible travel in Iceland is choosing the right accommodation. Many hotels and guesthouses in Reykjavík and other major towns are equipped to accommodate guests with disabilities. When booking accommodations, it's essential to look for places that specifically mention accessibility features such as wheelchair ramps, elevators, and accessible bathrooms. Websites like Booking.com allow you to filter your search results for properties that cater to guests with disabilities. It's also a good idea to contact the accommodation directly to inquire about specific accessibility features, ensuring that your needs will be met during your stay. For those who prefer a more local experience, consider checking out Icelandic Airbnb listings, where you can often find homes that offer wheelchair access and other accommodations.

In Reykjavík, many attractions and public transportation options are designed with accessibility in mind. The city has made significant efforts to ensure that key tourist sites, such as the National Museum of Iceland, Harpa Concert Hall, and Hallgrímskirkja church, are accessible to all visitors. Most public buildings comply with accessibility standards, featuring ramps, elevators, and accessible restrooms. However, as you plan your itinerary, it's beneficial to check the specific accessibility features of each attraction beforehand. Many tourist sites have websites that outline their facilities for guests with disabilities, including information on parking, restroom accessibility, and guided tours.

When it comes to getting around, public transportation in Reykjavík is generally accessible. Buses are equipped with low floors and ramps, making it easier for wheelchair users or those with mobility challenges to board. The Reykjavík public transportation system operates under the Strætó brand, and their website offers information on routes and schedules, including details about accessibility. You can also download the Strætó app, which provides real-time information about bus arrivals and route planning. If you prefer a more direct mode of transportation, many taxi services in Iceland have accessible vehicles available upon request. It's a good idea to call ahead to ensure that the taxi you order has the necessary accommodations for your needs.

For those wishing to look around outside of Reykjavík, the accessibility of attractions can vary. Many popular natural sites, such as waterfalls, geysers, and hot springs, have made efforts to improve accessibility, but not all areas are fully equipped. For example, the Golden Circle route, which includes Þingvellir National Park, Gullfoss waterfall, and Geysir geothermal area, has some accessible paths and viewing platforms, but certain trails may be challenging. It's crucial to research each site beforehand to understand their accessibility options. The Icelandic Tourist Board provides information on accessible travel and attractions across the country, which can be a valuable resource for planning your trip.

If you plan to participate in guided tours or excursions, look for companies that specialize in accessible travel. Some tour operators in Iceland offer tailored experiences for guests with mobility challenges, ensuring that transportation and activities are designed with accessibility in mind. These operators often provide wheelchair-accessible vans and arrange visits to attractions that have proper facilities. It's important to communicate your needs when booking a tour, so the company can make the necessary arrangements and provide you with the best possible experience.

For outdoor enthusiasts, Iceland has several beautiful landscapes to look around, but navigating rugged terrain can be difficult. If you're interested in hiking or walking tours, consider looking for accessible trails or guided tours that focus on easier paths. Some locations, such as the Reynisfjara black sand beach, have accessible viewing areas, but be aware that the beach itself can be challenging due to loose sand and uneven surfaces. The Snaefellsnes Peninsula and various national parks offer stunning scenery, and while some paths may be accessible, others may require more advanced planning. Engaging with local guides who are knowledgeable about accessibility can help ensure that you make the most of your outdoor adventures.

Another critical aspect of accessible travel in Iceland is the weather. The country is known for its unpredictable weather, and conditions can change quickly, especially in the highlands and coastal areas. Before heading out for any outdoor activities or excursions, make sure to check the weather forecast and dress appropriately. Layering is key, as temperatures can vary significantly throughout the day. Comfortable, waterproof footwear is essential for keeping your feet dry, particularly when exploring areas where paths may be wet or muddy.

In terms of health and safety, tourists should be aware of the importance of having travel insurance that covers potential medical needs. While Iceland has a high standard of healthcare, it's always best to be prepared for unexpected situations. Make sure your insurance covers emergency evacuation, especially if you plan to look around more remote areas where access to medical facilities may be limited. It's also a good idea to carry a small first aid kit, including necessary medications and any mobility aids you may require.

Finally, when dining out in Iceland, many restaurants and cafes are accommodating and have made efforts to ensure accessibility for all patrons. Most establishments in Reykjavík offer a range of dining options, and many are equipped with ramps and accessible restrooms. If you have specific dietary needs or require assistance, it's beneficial to communicate this to the staff. In Iceland, restaurant staff are generally friendly and willing to help ensure that your dining experience is enjoyable.

CHAPTER 7

WHAT TO DO: ACTIVITIES FOR EVERY TRAVELER

Activities for Different Types of Travelers

Iceland is a stunning destination that offers a variety of activities suitable for different types of travelers, including those with accessibility needs. Whether you are an adventurous look around, a family with children, or someone who prefers a more leisurely pace, Iceland has something for everyone. It is essential for visitors to understand the available accessible activities that allow them to experience the beauty of this unique landscape, while also accommodating their individual needs.

For travelers seeking adventure, Iceland's natural wonders provide countless opportunities for exploration. Many tour companies offer accessible excursions that allow individuals with mobility challenges to enjoy the breathtaking scenery. For instance, the famous Golden Circle route is a popular choice, featuring highlights such as Þingvellir National Park, Geysir geothermal area, and Gullfoss waterfall. While some areas within these sites may have rough terrain, many tour operators have adapted their vehicles and itineraries to ensure access for all travelers. Buses with low floors and ramps are available, and paths leading to key viewpoints are often paved or well-maintained. Tours may also include accessible walking paths and viewing platforms, allowing everyone to enjoy the incredible sights without the need for strenuous hiking.

Another popular activity for adventurous travelers is exploring Iceland's glaciers. Some companies offer guided glacier hikes with accessibility options. These tours typically use specialized equipment, such as ice grips or wheelchairs designed for snowy conditions, to make glacier exploration more feasible for individuals with mobility issues. Participants can experience the stunning ice formations and glacial landscapes in a safe and enjoyable manner. It is essential to book these tours with companies that have experience providing accessible options, as they will ensure that safety measures are in place.

For those interested in wildlife, Iceland is renowned for its puffins and whales. Whale-watching tours often provide accessible boats designed to accommodate travelers with mobility challenges. These tours allow participants to enjoy the beauty of the ocean while watching whales and other marine life in their natural habitat. Many operators offer guidance on accessibility features, such as wheelchair ramps and designated seating areas, ensuring that everyone can partake in the adventure. Similarly, puffin-watching tours, particularly those that take place on accessible islands, provide a unique opportunity to observe these charming birds in their nesting habitats.

Cultural experiences are also abundant in Iceland, offering something for every type of traveler. Museums and cultural centers, such as the National Museum of Iceland and the Reykjavík Art Museum, generally prioritize accessibility. These institutions often feature ramps, elevators, and accessible restrooms, making it easy for visitors with mobility needs to enjoy the exhibits. Many museums offer guided tours that can be tailored to accommodate specific accessibility requirements, providing deeper insights into Icelandic history and culture.

For those seeking a more relaxed experience, geothermal hot springs are a quintessential part of Icelandic culture. While some hot springs may have limited accessibility, many popular sites, like the Blue Lagoon, are designed with inclusivity in mind. The Blue Lagoon features ramps, accessible changing rooms, and wheelchair-friendly paths, allowing everyone to experience the therapeutic waters. Other geothermal pools, such as the Secret Lagoon in Flúðir, also offer accessible facilities, making it easy to enjoy a soak in nature. Before visiting, it's wise to check the specific accessibility options available at each location, as some pools may have varying levels of accessibility.

If you are traveling with children or family members, there are numerous family-friendly activities available in Iceland that also cater to different accessibility needs. One popular option is visiting family-oriented attractions like the Reykjavík Zoo and Family Park, where visitors of all ages can enjoy petting zoos, playgrounds, and various animals. The park is designed to be accessible, with pathways suitable for strollers and wheelchair users, allowing families to spend a fun day together without barriers. Similarly, places like

Laugardalslaug, one of the largest swimming pools in Reykjavík, offer family-friendly amenities, including shallow areas for younger children and accessible entry points for those with mobility challenges.

For those interested in local cuisine, many restaurants in Iceland are accommodating. While dining out, travelers with accessibility needs can find restaurants that offer wheelchair access and accessible seating. It's advisable to call ahead to confirm accessibility features, especially during busy dining hours. Icelandic cuisine offers a range of traditional dishes, and many restaurants are willing to cater to dietary restrictions or preferences. Enjoying local food is an important part of the travel experience, and most establishments are eager to ensure that everyone can enjoy a meal.

In addition to activities that promote exploration and cultural immersion, Iceland also offers opportunities for relaxation and rejuvenation. Accessible wellness retreats and spas are available, focusing on providing relaxing experiences for individuals with mobility challenges. Many wellness centers prioritize inclusivity by offering specialized treatments and accessible facilities. Taking time to relax and recharge in a tranquil environment is a vital part of enjoying a trip, and Iceland's serene landscapes provide the perfect backdrop for relaxation.

Traveling in Iceland is made easier by the country's efficient public transportation system, particularly in Reykjavík. The buses are designed to accommodate passengers with disabilities, featuring low floors and ramps. This makes it easier for travelers with mobility devices to find your way the city and reach various attractions. Moreover, many popular tourist destinations are located close to public transport routes, making it convenient for travelers to look around without the need for a rental car. It's also possible to arrange for accessible taxis that are equipped to handle wheelchairs, ensuring that getting around is as smooth as possible.

Planning ahead is key to enjoying accessible activities in Iceland. Researching potential destinations, activities, and accommodations before your trip will help ensure that you are well-prepared for any challenges that may arise. Many tour operators and businesses in Iceland are happy to accommodate special requests, so don't hesitate to reach out in advance to discuss your specific needs. Additionally, consider connecting with local organizations or travel agencies that specialize in accessible travel; they can offer invaluable insights and recommendations tailored to your interests.

Day Trips and Excursions

Iceland is a country rich in natural beauty, diverse landscapes, and unique experiences, making it an ideal destination for day trips and excursions. For travelers eager to look around the stunning scenery, fascinating culture, and incredible geology, there are numerous organized tours and self-guided options available. These excursions allow visitors to immerse themselves in Iceland's extraordinary environments, from the famous Golden Circle to the captivating South Coast and beyond. Knowing the best day trips to take, what to expect, and how to plan can greatly enhance your travel experience in this remarkable country.

One of the most popular day trips is the Golden Circle, a route that showcases some of Iceland's most iconic natural wonders. This loop covers approximately 300 kilometers and includes three main attractions: Þingvellir National Park, the Geysir geothermal area, and Gullfoss waterfall. Þingvellir is a UNESCO World Heritage Site, known for its stunning rift valley that marks the boundary between the North American and Eurasian tectonic plates. Visitors can walk through the park, exploring its unique geology and rich history as the site of Iceland's first parliament. Guided tours typically include transportation from Reykjavík, making it easy for tourists to visit these remarkable sites in one day.

The Geysir geothermal area is another highlight of the Golden Circle. Here, travelers can witness Strokkur, a geyser that erupts every few minutes, shooting water up to 30 meters into the air. The geothermal landscape is dotted with hot springs, mud pots, and fumaroles, providing a captivating glimpse into the Earth's geothermal activity. After visiting Geysir, the next stop is Gullfoss, one of Iceland's most magnificent waterfalls. The water cascades down two tiers, creating a breathtaking view that captivates visitors. Many tour operators offer combined Golden Circle tours that include lunch and additional stops, such as the Fridheimar greenhouse, where you can learn about Icelandic farming practices and taste delicious tomato-based dishes.

For those interested in the South Coast, a day trip along this route offers spectacular scenery, including waterfalls, black sand beaches, and glaciers. Two of the most famous waterfalls on the South Coast are Seljalandsfoss and Skógafoss. Seljalandsfoss is unique because visitors can walk behind the waterfall, providing a thrilling perspective and excellent photo opportunities. Skógafoss, on the other hand, is one of the largest waterfalls in Iceland, with a drop of 60 meters. The mist created by the waterfall often results in rainbows on sunny days, adding to its beauty.

A popular stop along the South Coast is Reynisfjara beach, famous for its black sand, striking basalt columns, and dramatic sea stacks. The beach is located near the town of Vík, where visitors can enjoy stunning coastal views. However, caution is advised when visiting Reynisfjara, as the waves can be unpredictable and dangerous. It's essential to stay a safe distance from the water and heed any warnings from local authorities or tour guides. Many day tours along the South Coast include opportunities for glacier hiking or ice climbing on Sólheimajökull, a glacier outlet of Mýrdalsjökull. This is a fantastic way for adventurous travelers to experience the beauty of Iceland's glaciers up close.

For those wanting to venture further, a day trip to Snæfellsnes Peninsula is highly recommended. Often referred to as "Iceland in Miniature," this area features a diverse range of landscapes, including mountains, waterfalls, beaches, and lava fields. A highlight of the peninsula is Snæfellsjökull National Park, home to the Snæfellsjökull glacier-capped volcano. Visitors can look around hiking trails, lava tubes, and scenic viewpoints. The picturesque village of Arnarstapi and the dramatic rock formations at Gatklettur are also must-see sites along the way. Many guided tours from Reykjavík include transportation, allowing tourists to fully enjoy the scenery without the hassle of driving.

Wildlife enthusiasts will find that Iceland offers unique opportunities for spotting wildlife, particularly during the summer months. One of the most popular day trips is whale watching from Reykjavík or Akureyri. The waters surrounding Iceland are home to a variety of whale species, including minke whales, humpback whales, and even orcas. Many tour operators offer whale watching excursions, which often include knowledgeable guides who provide insights into marine life and the ecosystem. These tours usually last a few hours, and while sightings can't be guaranteed, many travelers leave with unforgettable memories and stunning photographs of these majestic creatures.

For travelers interested in Iceland's geothermal wonders, a visit to the Blue Lagoon is a must. While not a traditional day trip, many people incorporate a visit to this famous geothermal spa into their travel itinerary. Located about 20 minutes from Keflavík Airport, the Blue Lagoon features milky blue waters rich in minerals that are known for their healing properties. Visitors can relax in the warm waters, enjoy treatments at the spa, and dine at the on-site restaurant. It's advisable to book tickets in advance, as the Blue Lagoon can get busy, especially during peak tourist seasons. Many travelers choose to combine a visit to the Blue Lagoon with their arrival or departure flights, making it a convenient stop during their trip.

Self-guided excursions are also a popular option for travelers who prefer to look around at their own pace. Renting a car allows for flexibility and the ability to find out hidden gems along the way. Iceland's Ring Road, which encircles the country, offers breathtaking views and access to numerous attractions. However, it's important for travelers to plan their routes carefully, especially when venturing into more remote areas. Many websites and travel blogs provide detailed itineraries and recommendations for self-driving trips, including suggested stops and estimated travel times.

Regardless of the type of excursion you choose, it's essential to be well-prepared. Weather in Iceland can change rapidly, so wearing layers and bringing waterproof clothing is crucial. Comfortable shoes are also a must, especially if you plan on walking or hiking during your day trips. It's a good idea to bring snacks and water, as some attractions may be in remote areas where access to food and drink is limited. Additionally, for those traveling with children or individuals with accessibility needs, contacting tour operators in advance to discuss specific requirements can help ensure a smooth experience.

Guided Nature Walks

Guided nature walks in Iceland offer a unique and immersive way to experience the country's stunning landscapes, rich biodiversity, and fascinating geology. With its dramatic scenery, from towering waterfalls and vast lava fields to serene hot springs and vibrant moss-covered hills, Iceland is a paradise for nature enthusiasts. A guided nature walk allows visitors to look around these beautiful environments while benefiting from the knowledge and expertise of experienced guides who can enhance the experience with insights about the local flora, fauna, and geology.

One of the key advantages of participating in guided nature walks is the opportunity to access areas that might be difficult to find your way independently. Iceland's terrain can be rugged and unpredictable, and the weather can change rapidly. Knowledgeable guides know the safest and most interesting routes, ensuring that participants can enjoy the beauty of the landscapes without the stress of getting lost or facing challenging conditions. Many guided walks are designed to cater to various skill levels, from leisurely strolls suitable for families to more strenuous hikes for those seeking a challenge. This inclusivity makes guided walks accessible to a wide range of travelers, regardless of their experience or fitness level.

One of the most popular areas for guided nature walks is Þingvellir National Park, a UNESCO World Heritage Site known for its stunning landscapes and historical significance. Visitors can look around the rift valley created by the tectonic plates pulling apart, which offers unique geological features, including fissures and volcanic landscapes. Guided walks in Þingvellir often include opportunities to learn about the park's cultural heritage, including its role in Iceland's early parliament and its significance to the Icelandic people. Experienced guides can point out the diverse plant life, including the rare and beautiful Arctic birch, and explain the park's geology, which provides fascinating insights into the Earth's processes.

Another popular location for guided nature walks is the South Coast, where stunning waterfalls, glaciers, and black sand beaches await. One of the highlights is the chance to visit the breathtaking Seljalandsfoss and Skógafoss waterfalls. A guided walk in this region may include routes that lead behind the cascading water of Seljalandsfoss, providing a unique perspective of the falls while learning about the geology and hydrology of the area. Skógafoss, one of Iceland's largest waterfalls, offers a dramatic backdrop for guided tours that often extend to the nearby Skógar Museum, where visitors can learn about traditional Icelandic culture and history.

The Snaefellsnes Peninsula, often referred to as "Iceland in Miniature," is another prime destination for guided nature walks. This region features diverse landscapes, including volcanic craters, coastal cliffs, and picturesque fishing villages. Guided walks here may include excursions to Snæfellsjökull National Park, home to the glacier-capped Snæfellsjökull volcano. Walks in this area can range from easy hikes to more challenging treks, with guides providing insights into the myths and legends associated with the region, such as the stories surrounding the "gateway to the center of the Earth." Travelers can also spot various bird species along the coastal cliffs, making it a rewarding experience for birdwatchers and nature lovers alike.

For those interested in exploring Iceland's geothermal areas, guided nature walks around the famous Geysir geothermal area are a must. These walks often include visits to Strokkur, a geyser that erupts every few minutes, along with smaller hot springs and bubbling mud pots. Knowledgeable guides can explain the geothermal activity in the region, the science behind geysers, and the various minerals that create the vibrant colors in the hot springs. The opportunity to learn about the cultural and historical significance of these geothermal features adds depth to the experience, making it both educational and enjoyable.

Glacier walking is another thrilling option offered by many guided tour companies in Iceland. Experienced guides take groups onto the stunning Sólheimajökull glacier, providing all the necessary equipment, such as crampons and ice axes. These walks typically begin with a safety briefing and an introduction to the glacier's unique features. Participants have the chance to look around ice caves, deep crevasses, and fascinating formations while learning about the effects of climate change on glaciers. This hands-on experience allows visitors to connect with the environment in a meaningful way and gain an understanding of the challenges facing these magnificent natural wonders.

For those who want a more relaxed experience, guided nature walks can also focus on birdwatching or photography. Many tour operators specialize in catering to photographers, providing guidance on the best locations for capturing stunning images of Iceland's landscapes, wildlife, and unique geological formations. Guided birdwatching tours allow participants to see a variety of species, including puffins, eider ducks, and Arctic terns, all while learning about their habitats and behaviors. Guides often have extensive knowledge of the local ecology and can help identify different birds and their calls, making these tours enriching for both novice and experienced birdwatchers.

When it comes to planning a guided nature walk in Iceland, booking in advance is often recommended, especially during the peak tourist season in the summer months. Many tour companies operate online, allowing travelers to easily check availability, compare prices, and read reviews from previous participants. It is essential to choose reputable companies that prioritize safety and sustainability. Reading through customer reviews can provide insights into the quality of the experience and the knowledge of the guides.

The price of guided nature walks can vary depending on the length of the tour, the destination, and the inclusivity of services provided. Shorter walks may cost around $50 to $100 USD per person, while more extensive full-day hikes or specialized excursions, such as glacier walks or birdwatching tours, can range from $100 to $250 USD or more. It's important to consider what is included in the price, such as transportation, equipment rental, and meals, to determine the overall value of the experience.

Travelers should also be aware of the physical demands of guided nature walks. While many tours are designed to be accessible, it's still essential to choose walks that match your fitness level and experience. It's advisable to wear appropriate clothing and footwear, as weather conditions in Iceland can change quickly. Layering is key, along with waterproof and windproof outer layers. Comfortable hiking boots with good grip will make the experience more enjoyable, especially when traversing rocky or uneven terrain.

Popular Walking and Hiking Trails

Iceland is renowned for its breathtaking landscapes, making it a paradise for walking and hiking enthusiasts. The country offers a wide range of trails that showcase its diverse natural beauty, from dramatic coastlines and glacial vistas to green valleys and volcanic terrain.

One of the most famous hiking routes in Iceland is the Laugavegur Trail, often considered the crown jewel of Icelandic trekking. This approximately 55-kilometer (34-mile) trail runs from Landmannalaugar to Þórsmörk, taking hikers through a stunning variety of landscapes, including colorful rhyolite mountains, geothermal hot springs, and expansive glaciers. The trail typically takes around four to six days to complete, depending on the pace and the chosen itinerary. Each section of the hike reveals a different aspect of Iceland's natural beauty, with highlights such as the vibrant geothermal area at Landmannalaugar, where you can soak in hot springs after a day of hiking. The route is well-marked, and hikers can find huts or camping sites along the way, making it accessible even for those who prefer not to carry heavy gear. However, it is essential to plan ahead, as the trail can be crowded during the peak summer months, and reservations for huts should be made in advance.

Another popular trail is the Glymur Waterfall hike, located in Hvalfjörður, just north of Reykjavík. This trail is approximately 7 kilometers (4.3 miles) round trip and leads to Glymur, one of Iceland's tallest waterfalls, with a height of 198 meters (650 feet). The hike to Glymur is relatively moderate and offers stunning views of the surrounding fjord and green vegetation. Along the way, hikers will find your way a variety of terrains, including rocky paths and small stream crossings, which add to the adventure. The final stretch offers an opportunity to walk along a narrow ledge, providing a thrilling view of the waterfall below. This trail can usually be completed in about 3 to 4 hours and is particularly popular among families and day-trippers from Reykjavík.

For those seeking a coastal experience, the Skaftafell National Park area offers various hiking trails that showcase Iceland's unique glacial landscapes. One of the most popular hikes within the park is to Svartifoss, also known as the Black Waterfall. This approximately 5.5-kilometer (3.4-mile) round trip trail leads hikers through green birch woods and along glacial rivers before arriving at the striking waterfall, which is surrounded by dark basalt columns that resemble organ pipes. The hike to Svartifoss typically takes around 1.5 to 2 hours, making it an accessible option for families and casual walkers. Skaftafell National Park also provides more challenging trails, including routes leading up to the glacier tongue of Vatnajökull, Europe's largest glacier. Experienced hikers can join guided glacier walks that allow them to look around the ice formations and crevasses safely.

The Fimmvörðuháls Trail is another exceptional hiking route, stretching approximately 25 kilometers (15.5 miles) between Skógar and Þórsmörk. This trail is known for its breathtaking views of waterfalls, including the famous Skógafoss, and the stunning landscape between two glaciers: Eyjafjallajökull and Mýrdalsjökull. The hike typically takes around 8 to 10 hours, and while it is more strenuous than some other options, the scenery is absolutely worth the effort. The trail showcases Iceland's volcanic activity and diverse ecosystems, including green green valleys, wildflower meadows, and rocky terrains. Hikers should be prepared for changing weather conditions, as the elevation changes significantly along the route, and it's advisable to wear sturdy footwear and layered clothing.

For a more leisurely stroll, the Reykjavík coastal path offers a beautiful walking experience without venturing far from the capital city. This scenic pathway stretches about 10 kilometers (6.2 miles) along the coastline, providing stunning views of the ocean, mountains, and city skyline. It connects various parks, beaches, and public artworks, making it an ideal choice for families or those looking to enjoy a casual walk. Along the way, walkers can enjoy landmarks such as the Harpa Concert Hall, the Sun Voyager sculpture, and picturesque views of Mount Esja across the bay. This route is accessible year-round and is a great way to experience the local culture while enjoying the fresh air.

For those interested in experiencing Iceland's unique geological formations, the Hveradalir geothermal area in Kerlingarfjöll is a must-visit. The hiking trails in this area vary in difficulty, but they all provide access to bubbling hot springs, vibrant colored earth, and steam vents. The landscapes are otherworldly, with the geothermal activity showcasing a range of colors from red to yellow to green, thanks to the minerals present in the soil. Hikes can range from easy walks to more challenging routes that lead into the surrounding mountains. Travelers often report feeling like they are walking on another planet, given the stark contrasts between the geothermal areas and the rugged terrain.

Iceland's natural beauty also offers opportunities for unique experiences such as lava field hikes. The Eldhraun Lava Field, formed during an eruption in the late 18th century, is one of the largest lava fields in the world and provides an intriguing landscape to look around. Hikers can traverse this surreal terrain, characterized by soft moss-covered lava formations and unique rock structures. Guided tours in this area can provide valuable context about the volcanic activity that shaped Iceland's landscapes.

When planning hiking excursions, it is crucial to consider safety precautions and prepare adequately. Weather conditions in Iceland can change rapidly, and even in summer, temperatures can be cool and windy. Wearing layered clothing is essential to adapt to changing conditions, and sturdy, waterproof hiking boots are highly recommended. Hikers should also carry plenty of water and snacks, as well as a basic first aid kit for emergencies. Always let someone know your plans and expected return time if you're hiking in more remote areas, and consider using a GPS or a map to ensure you stay on track.

For those who wish to join guided hiking tours, numerous companies offer a variety of options across the country, catering to different fitness levels and interests. Booking in advance is advisable, especially during the peak summer season when trails can be busy. Many tour operators provide equipment such as crampons and walking poles for glacier hikes, ensuring a safe and enjoyable experience.

Local Adventure Sports

Iceland is a breathtaking country known for its stunning landscapes, and it has become a popular destination for adventure sports enthusiasts from around the world. The unique geological features and diverse natural environments make it an ideal playground for those seeking thrilling experiences. From ice climbing on glaciers to exploring lava caves and white-water rafting through rugged rivers, Iceland offers a wide range of adventure sports that cater to different skill levels and interests.

With its many glaciers, including Vatnajökull, the largest glacier in Europe, and Sólheimajökull, glacier hiking allows participants to look around these magnificent ice formations up close. Guided glacier hikes typically involve a professional guide who provides all necessary equipment, including crampons and ice axes, ensuring a safe and enjoyable experience. These hikes can vary in difficulty, with some suitable for beginners and others designed for more experienced climbers. The breathtaking views from the glaciers, including deep crevasses, ice caves, and seracs, create a stunning backdrop for unforgettable photographs. Many tour operators offer half-day or full-day glacier hikes, often combined with additional activities such as ice climbing or exploring ice caves.

Another thrilling activity is ice climbing, which takes glacier hiking to the next level. This sport involves ascending vertical ice formations using specialized gear, including ice axes and crampons. Ice climbing in Iceland typically takes place on glaciers, where climbers can find various routes suited to their skill level. Experienced guides provide instruction and support, making it accessible for beginners who are looking to try something new. Ice climbing tours often include all necessary equipment, so participants do not need to bring their own gear. The feeling of scaling a glacier while surrounded by towering ice walls is an Exciting experience that many adventure seekers cherish.

Caving and exploring lava tubes are also popular adventure activities in Iceland. The country's volcanic landscape has created numerous lava tubes, formed when lava flows beneath the surface and cools, leaving behind hollow tunnels. One of the most famous lava tubes is the Leidarendi cave, located near Reykjavík. Guided tours of these caves allow visitors to find out stunning rock formations, stalactites, and stalagmites while learning about the geological processes that created them. Caving tours can vary in length, typically lasting from a few hours to a full day, and are suitable for people of all ages. Safety gear, such as helmets and headlamps, is provided, ensuring that participants can safely enjoy the exploration of these fascinating underground landscapes.

For those who crave speed and excitement, snowmobiling on glaciers offers an adrenaline-pumping experience. This activity allows adventurers to zip across the vast ice fields of Iceland, taking in the breathtaking scenery while experiencing the thrill of riding a snowmobile. Tours are typically guided and include all necessary equipment, along with safety instructions. Snowmobiling on glaciers provides a unique perspective on the icy terrain and allows travelers to access areas that would otherwise be difficult to reach. The combination of speed, stunning views, and the unique landscape makes snowmobiling a memorable adventure for anyone visiting Iceland during the winter months.

Kayaking is another adventure sport that allows visitors to experience Iceland's stunning coastline and tranquil fjords from a unique vantage point. Sea kayaking tours are available in various locations, including Reykjavík and the Westfjords, where paddlers can look around hidden coves, observe marine wildlife, and enjoy the beautiful scenery. These tours often cater to different skill levels, from beginners to experienced kayakers. Participants can encounter puffins, seals, and other wildlife, making it a rewarding experience for nature lovers. Guided kayaking tours typically provide all necessary equipment and safety gear, as well as instruction for those new to the sport.

For thrill-seekers looking for a rush of adrenaline, white-water rafting in Iceland's rivers is an exciting option. The country offers some fantastic rafting experiences, particularly in the Þjórsá River and the Hvítá River. These rivers feature various sections, from calm waters perfect for beginners to more challenging rapids for experienced rafters. Guided rafting tours provide participants with all necessary safety equipment and trained guides who ensure a safe and enjoyable adventure. Rafting through Iceland's stunning landscapes, surrounded by mountains and waterfalls, adds to the excitement and creates lasting memories.

Hiking in Iceland can also be considered an adventure sport, as the country boasts a wide array of trails that vary in difficulty and terrain. Many of these trails take hikers through spectacular landscapes, including volcanic craters, geothermal areas, and breathtaking waterfalls. Popular hiking routes, such as the Laugavegur Trail and the

Fimmvörðuháls Trail, offer multi-day trekking experiences for those looking to immerse themselves in Iceland's natural beauty. Guided hiking tours often include experienced guides who provide valuable insights into the geography, flora, and fauna of the area, enhancing the hiking experience for participants.

For those interested in horseback riding, Icelandic horses are known for their unique gait and friendly demeanor. Riding tours are available throughout the country, allowing participants to look around scenic landscapes on horseback. Riders of all skill levels can enjoy these tours, which often take place in stunning locations such as the Þingvellir National Park or the beaches of Reynisfjara. The slow-paced, guided rides offer an excellent opportunity to experience Iceland's natural beauty while connecting with these charming animals.

When planning adventure sports in Iceland, it's essential to consider the time of year and weather conditions. The summer months, from June to August, are popular for hiking and outdoor activities due to the milder weather and longer daylight hours. However, winter offers unique opportunities for snow-related activities, such as glacier hikes, snowmobiling, and ice climbing. Regardless of the season, it is crucial to check weather forecasts and be prepared for changing conditions. Dressing in layers, wearing appropriate footwear, and bringing waterproof clothing are essential for enjoying outdoor activities comfortably.

Safety should always be a top priority when participating in adventure sports. It is essential to choose reputable tour operators who prioritize safety and follow industry guidelines. Most adventure sports require participants to sign a waiver or acknowledgment of risk, which is standard practice. It's also a good idea to inform guides of any medical conditions or concerns before starting an activity, as this allows them to accommodate your needs effectively.

Local Boat Tours and Cruises

Iceland is renowned for its stunning landscapes, and one of the best ways to experience its natural beauty is through local boat tours and cruises. These excursions allow tourists to look around the country's breathtaking coastline, picturesque fjords, and diverse marine life while enjoying unique views that are often only accessible from the water. With various options available, from whale watching and puffin tours to glacier cruises and fishing trips, there is something for everyone looking to start on a maritime adventure in Iceland.

One of the most popular types of boat tours in Iceland is whale watching. The waters surrounding Iceland are rich in marine life, making it one of the best places in the world for observing whales. Numerous tour companies operate from various coastal towns, with Reykjavík, Akureyri, and Húsavík being the most popular departure points. Húsavík, in particular, is often referred to as the whale watching capital of Iceland. Many boat tours from Húsavík offer exceptional opportunities to see species such as minke whales, humpback whales, and even orcas. Tours typically last around 2 to 3 hours, during which knowledgeable guides provide information about the whales, their behaviors, and the marine ecosystem. Whale watching tours generally run from April to October, with the peak season occurring during the summer months when whale activity is at its highest.

In addition to whale watching, many tours offer the chance to observe puffins, especially during the breeding season from late April to mid-August. Puffin tours often take place on small boats that can find your way closer to the cliffs where these colorful birds nest. The vibrant beaks of puffins make them a favorite for wildlife photographers and birdwatchers alike. Tours to islands like Akurey and Lundey, located just a short boat ride from Reykjavík, are popular spots for puffin viewing. Guides share insights about puffin habits, their migratory patterns, and their unique adaptations, enriching the experience for participants.

Glacier cruises are another exceptional way to look around Iceland's unique landscapes. Several companies operate tours in and around Jökulsárlón Glacier Lagoon, one of Iceland's most famous attractions. This stunning glacial lagoon is filled with icebergs that have broken off from the nearby Breiðamerkurjökull glacier. Boat tours in the lagoon allow visitors to get up close to these majestic ice formations and often provide opportunities to see seals swimming in the water. The experience of gliding through the icy waters surrounded by towering icebergs is truly unforgettable. Many tours also include a visit to the nearby Diamond Beach, where chunks of ice wash up on the black sand, creating a stark contrast that is perfect for photography.

In addition to Jökulsárlón, the nearby Fjallsárlón is another beautiful glacier lagoon that offers a more intimate experience away from the crowds. Here, smaller boat tours are available, allowing participants to look around the lagoon's serene waters and enjoy the peaceful surroundings. Guides often share information about the glacier's movement and the environmental changes affecting these stunning landscapes.

Fishing trips are another popular option for tourists looking to experience Iceland's rich marine resources. Many local fishing tours depart from coastal towns, allowing participants to try their hand at catching a variety of fish, including cod, haddock, and pollock. These trips often cater to all skill levels, from beginners to seasoned anglers. Equipment is typically provided, and local guides share their expertise on fishing techniques, the best spots to catch fish, and the regulations surrounding fishing in Icelandic waters. The experience of fishing in the pristine waters surrounding Iceland, combined with the breathtaking views, makes for a memorable day on the ocean.

For those looking for a more leisurely experience, dinner cruises provide a unique way to enjoy Icelandic cuisine while taking in the beautiful coastal scenery. Many companies offer evening cruises in Reykjavík, where guests can savor delicious meals while sailing around the bay. These cruises often feature fresh seafood dishes made with local ingredients, allowing visitors to experience the culinary delights of Iceland while enjoying the picturesque views of the city skyline and surrounding mountains. Some dinner cruises even include live music or entertainment, enhancing the overall experience.

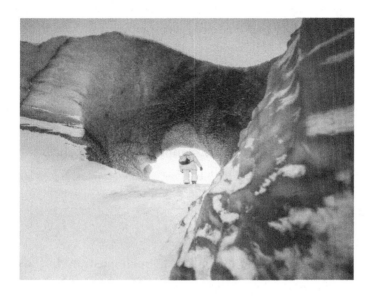

When planning a boat tour or cruise in Iceland, it is essential to consider the time of year and the weather conditions. The summer months, from June to August, generally offer the best weather for outdoor activities, including boat tours. However, it is always wise to check the forecast and be prepared for changing conditions, as weather in Iceland can be unpredictable. Dressing in layers and wearing waterproof clothing is advisable, especially if you are going on a boat trip where you may encounter splashes from waves or sudden changes in weather.

Booking boat tours in advance is recommended, particularly during the peak tourist season when popular excursions can fill up quickly. Many tour operators allow online bookings, making it easy to secure your spot before your trip. Additionally, reading reviews and comparing different operators can help you choose a reputable company that prioritizes safety and customer satisfaction.

Safety is a top priority on all boat tours, and reputable companies adhere to strict safety regulations. Life jackets are typically provided, and crews are trained in emergency procedures. It's essential to follow any safety instructions given by the guides and to communicate any concerns you may have before the tour begins.

Fishing Spots and Regulations

Fishing in Iceland is not only a popular pastime but also a deeply ingrained part of the country's culture and economy. The country boasts an abundance of pristine rivers, lakes, and coastal waters that offer fantastic opportunities for both freshwater and saltwater fishing. For tourists looking to cast a line, understanding the best fishing spots, regulations, and practices is essential for an enjoyable and successful fishing experience.

Iceland is renowned for its rich and diverse fish populations. In freshwater, you can find species such as salmon, trout, and char, while saltwater fishing offers opportunities to catch cod, haddock, and other species. One of the most famous fishing destinations in Iceland is the Laxa River in Aðaldalur, known for its exceptional salmon fishing. The river flows through beautiful landscapes, providing not only excellent fishing opportunities but also stunning views. Anglers can fish for salmon from June to September, with peak months being July and August. The river is accessible and has several fishing lodges nearby that cater to both novice and experienced anglers.

Another popular freshwater fishing location is Þingvallavatn, the largest natural lake in Iceland, situated in Þingvellir National Park. This lake is famous for its crystal-clear waters and abundant stocks of arctic char and brown trout. Fishing in Þingvallavatn is allowed year-round, but the best fishing typically occurs from late spring to early autumn. Anglers can find various spots around the lake, and many choose to rent a boat to access the deeper waters where larger fish are often found. The scenic surroundings make it a peaceful and picturesque place to fish.

For those interested in saltwater fishing, Reykjavík's harbor is a popular starting point for various fishing tours. Many local operators offer excursions that allow tourists to experience the thrill of catching cod, haddock, and even the elusive pollock. These trips often last several hours and include all necessary equipment, as well as knowledgeable guides who can help with techniques and tips for successful fishing. The best time for saltwater fishing in Iceland is during the summer months when the fish are more active. Common methods include bottom fishing and jigging, which can be learned quickly, making this a great option for beginners.

When planning to fish in Iceland, it is crucial to be aware of the regulations governing fishing activities. The Icelandic government regulates fishing to protect fish populations and maintain sustainable practices. Different fishing areas have specific rules regarding licenses, quotas, and seasons, which must be followed. For freshwater fishing, an official fishing license is required, which can usually be purchased from local fishing associations or online through various tour operators. The licenses often come with specific terms, such as catch limits and designated fishing spots. Adhering to these regulations is vital for the conservation of fish species and the environment.

For salmon fishing, many rivers require the purchase of a special salmon fishing license, which often includes a daily or weekly fee. These licenses are limited to ensure sustainable practices, and anglers are encouraged to practice catch and release when possible. Some rivers are privately owned, and access may be limited to those who have purchased licenses from the landowners or local associations. Therefore, it is essential to plan ahead and research the specific river or area where you intend to fish to ensure compliance with local regulations.

For trout fishing, the regulations can vary depending on the region and specific water bodies. Some lakes and rivers allow fishing year-round, while others have designated open seasons. Again, obtaining the proper fishing license is necessary, and anglers should always check the local guidelines for the specific area they plan to visit. In general, Iceland promotes sustainable fishing practices, and many guides will emphasize the importance of handling fish carefully to minimize stress and promote survival after release.

Fishing gear and equipment can be rented from local shops or tour operators if you do not want to bring your own. Many fishing tours include all necessary equipment, making it easy for tourists to participate without the hassle of packing bulky gear. For those who prefer to fish independently, local shops offer everything from rods and reels to bait and tackle. The staff in these shops are often very knowledgeable about local fishing conditions and can provide helpful advice on where to fish and what techniques to use.

Aside from the practical aspects, fishing in Iceland also provides an opportunity to connect with the country's stunning landscapes and vibrant ecosystems. Many fishing spots are located in remote areas, allowing visitors to experience the tranquility of Iceland's nature. Whether you're fishing in a peaceful lake surrounded by mountains or on the rugged coastline with waves crashing nearby, the environment adds to the overall experience. The chance to spot wildlife, such as birds and seals, while fishing further enhances the adventure.

CHAPTER 8

FOOD, DINING, AND LOCAL CUISINE

Dining (for different travelers)

Dining in Iceland offers a rich culinary experience that reflects the country's unique geography, culture, and history. As a traveler in Iceland, you will encounter a variety of dining options that cater to different tastes and budgets, from traditional Icelandic fare to international cuisine. The country's restaurants and eateries often emphasize fresh, locally sourced ingredients, making dining an integral part of the Icelandic experience.

For those who want to savor traditional Icelandic cuisine, numerous restaurants offer dishes that showcase the country's culinary heritage. One of the most iconic dishes is hákarl, which is fermented shark. This dish has a strong flavor and is often served with a shot of Brennivín, a traditional Icelandic schnapps. While it may be an acquired taste, trying hákarl is considered a rite of passage for many visitors. You can find it in various traditional restaurants, especially in Reykjavík, where chefs may offer it as part of a tasting menu featuring other local specialties.

Another staple of Icelandic cuisine is lamb, which is known for its tenderness and flavor. Icelandic lamb is free-range and often grazes on the country's green grasses and wild herbs, contributing to its unique taste. Many restaurants serve roasted lamb dishes, often accompanied by seasonal vegetables. Additionally, seafood is a highlight of the Icelandic diet, with fresh catches coming directly from the surrounding waters. Dishes such as pan-seared fish, fish stew, and traditional fish soup are commonly found on menus. Restaurants near the coast, especially in fishing towns like Ísafjörður or Seyðisfjörður, often showcase the best of local seafood, with chefs creating dishes that celebrate the freshness and quality of the catch.

For travelers looking for casual dining options, Iceland has a growing number of cafés and bistros that offer a more relaxed atmosphere. These places often serve a range of light meals, such as sandwiches, salads, and pastries. Many cafés feature skyr, a traditional Icelandic dairy product that is thick and creamy, similar to yogurt. Skyr is often served with fruit or granola and is a delicious option for breakfast or a snack. Popular café chains like Kaffitár and Sandholt in Reykjavík are great places to sample local pastries, such as kleina (a twisted doughnut) or pönnukökur (Icelandic pancakes).

If you're a vegetarian or vegan traveler, you'll be pleased to know that Iceland has made strides in offering plant-based dining options. Many restaurants now include vegetarian and vegan dishes on their menus, reflecting the growing demand for diverse dietary choices. In Reykjavík, you can find dedicated vegetarian and vegan restaurants like Glo, which serves health-conscious meals made from fresh ingredients, and Kaffi Vegan for delicious plant-based comfort food. Additionally, many traditional restaurants are open to modifying dishes to accommodate dietary preferences, so don't hesitate to ask the staff for alternatives.

For those seeking fine dining experiences, Iceland offers several high-end restaurants that focus on innovative cuisine and artistic presentations. Dill, located in Reykjavík, has gained international acclaim for its use of Nordic ingredients and contemporary cooking techniques. The restaurant offers a tasting menu that changes with the seasons, showcasing the best local produce and seafood. Another noteworthy fine dining establishment is Matur og Drykkur, which takes a modern approach to traditional Icelandic dishes, combining local flavors with creative culinary techniques. Dining in these establishments provides not only a meal but also an opportunity to experience the artistry and creativity of Icelandic chefs.

When it comes to dining out in Iceland, it's essential to be aware of the local dining customs and practices. Reservations are recommended for popular restaurants, especially during the summer months when tourism peaks. Many restaurants have limited seating, and making a reservation ensures that you won't miss out on experiencing the best of Icelandic cuisine. Additionally, tipping is not customary in Iceland, as service charges are typically included in the bill. However, if you receive exceptional service, leaving a small tip is appreciated.

For a unique dining experience, consider trying one of the many food tours available in Iceland. These tours often include visits to various eateries, markets, and local producers, allowing you to sample a range of dishes and learn about the ingredients and traditions behind Icelandic cuisine. Food tours can provide a deeper understanding of the culinary culture, and they often highlight hidden gems that may not be on the average tourist's radar.

Shopping for local ingredients is also an exciting aspect of Icelandic dining. Many visitors enjoy exploring farmers' markets and local shops, where they can find traditional Icelandic products such as cured meats, cheeses, and artisanal bread. The Kolaportið Flea Market in Reykjavík is a popular spot to find out local foods, including fresh fish, baked goods, and homemade jams. Sampling local flavors from these markets can enhance your overall culinary experience in Iceland.

When dining in Iceland, be prepared for a range of prices. Fine dining establishments may charge higher prices for exquisite dishes and experiences, while more casual eateries offer reasonably priced options. It's advisable to check menus online or inquire about prices before dining, particularly if you're on a budget. Additionally, lunch menus at restaurants are often more affordable than dinner menus, making lunchtime a great opportunity to enjoy a nice meal at a lower cost.

Local Cuisine and Must-Try Dishes

Icelandic cuisine offers a unique culinary experience that reflects the country's history, culture, and natural resources. The cuisine is heavily influenced by Iceland's harsh climate and isolation, which have shaped traditional cooking methods and ingredient choices. When visiting Iceland, trying the local dishes is essential to fully appreciate the country's culture and heritage. The food here often features fresh, high-quality ingredients sourced from the land and sea, and it showcases a blend of traditional recipes and modern culinary techniques.

One of the most iconic dishes in Iceland is hákarl, or fermented shark. This dish is a true testament to Icelandic culture, as it has been consumed for centuries. Hákarl is made from Greenland shark, which is toxic when fresh due to high levels of urea and trimethylamine oxide. To make it safe for consumption, the shark is buried in the ground for several months, allowing it to ferment and decompose. The end product is a distinctive-smelling delicacy that is often served in small cubes. While it may be an acquired taste, many visitors find that trying hákarl is an essential part of their Icelandic experience. It is commonly accompanied by a shot of Brennivín, an Icelandic schnapps, which helps to wash down the strong flavor.

Another staple of Icelandic cuisine is lamb, which is known for its rich flavor. Icelandic lamb is free-range and grazes on the country's wild herbs and grasses, giving it a unique taste. Traditional dishes often include roasted lamb served with root vegetables and potatoes. One popular preparation is kjötsúpa, a hearty lamb soup made with vegetables and spices. This comforting dish is a favorite among locals, especially during the colder months, and it provides a warm and satisfying meal after a day of exploring the rugged landscapes.

Seafood plays a crucial role in Iceland's culinary offerings, thanks to the country's location in the North Atlantic Ocean. Fresh fish is a highlight of many menus, with cod, haddock, and salmon being among the most popular choices. One must-try dish is plokkfiskur, a traditional fish stew made from boiled fish, potatoes, onions, and a creamy sauce. This dish is often served with rye bread, and it is a comforting meal that showcases the fresh catch of the day. Another seafood delicacy is fish and chips, which is widely enjoyed across the country. Many restaurants serve their own versions of this classic dish, often using locally sourced fish for a fresher taste.

For those with a sweet tooth, Iceland offers delicious desserts that are not to be missed. One popular treat is skyr, a thick, yogurt-like dairy product that has been part of the Icelandic diet for over a thousand years. Skyr is high in protein and low in fat, making it a healthy option. It is often enjoyed plain or topped with fruit, honey, or granola. Additionally, Icelandic bakeries are known for their pastries, such as kleina, a twisted doughnut that is deep-fried and coated in sugar. These sweet treats can be found in cafés throughout the country and are a delightful way to experience Icelandic culture.

Icelandic cuisine also features unique breads, particularly rúgbrauð, a dense and dark rye bread. Traditionally, this bread was baked using geothermal heat, a method still practiced in some areas today. Rúgbrauð is often served with butter, smoked salmon, or pickled herring, and its rich flavor pairs well with various toppings. Many visitors enjoy sampling this bread during their travels, and some even participate in baking experiences where they can learn the traditional methods.

In addition to traditional dishes, Iceland's culinary scene has evolved in recent years, with many chefs embracing modern techniques and innovative flavors. Restaurants in Reykjavík and other urban areas often feature menus that showcase seasonal ingredients and creative preparations. For those interested in fine dining, places like Dill and Matur og Drykkur offer exceptional tasting menus that highlight Icelandic flavors through contemporary cooking styles. Dining at these establishments allows visitors to experience the artistry and creativity of Icelandic chefs who take pride in using local ingredients to craft unique dishes.

For travelers looking for a more casual dining experience, food trucks and street vendors are becoming increasingly popular in Iceland, particularly in Reykjavík. These vendors offer a variety of quick and tasty options, from traditional Icelandic hot dogs, known as pylsur, to gourmet street food inspired by international flavors. The Icelandic hot dog is a must-try, typically made from a blend of lamb, pork, and beef, and served with a variety of toppings, including crispy onions, raw onions, ketchup, and remoulade. The hot dog stands, particularly the famous Bæjarins Beztu Pylsur, are a popular choice for both locals and tourists looking for a quick bite.

When it comes to beverages, Iceland has a growing craft beer scene, with many breweries producing a wide range of local brews. Sampling Icelandic craft beer is a great way to complement your meals, and many restaurants and bars feature an impressive selection of local options. Additionally, traditional drinks such as schnapps and malt beer are commonly enjoyed, providing a taste of Icelandic culture. For non-alcoholic options, Icelandic soda, including brands like Appelsín (orange soda) and Malt (a malt beverage), can be refreshing choices, especially during warm weather.

It is essential for visitors to be aware of dining customs in Iceland. Tipping is not expected, as service charges are typically included in the bill, but rounding up the total or leaving small change for exceptional service is appreciated. Reservations are recommended for popular restaurants, especially during the busy summer months. Dining hours can vary, with many restaurants offering lunch from around 11 a.m. to 3 p.m. and dinner from 5 p.m. to 10 p.m., though some places may close earlier in the off-season.

CHAPTER 9

EXPLORING ICELAND'S CULTURE

Iceland is a land rich in culture and tradition, and its festivals and celebrations reflect the unique heritage and vibrant spirit of its people. Throughout the year, various events take place that highlight Icelandic history, folklore, and the changing seasons. These festivals provide visitors with an opportunity to immerse themselves in local culture, taste traditional foods, and participate in lively activities.

One of the most important festivals in Iceland is Þorrablót, which takes place in February and March. This midwinter festival celebrates the Viking heritage and honors the old traditions of feasting. The name Þorrablót translates to "sacrifice to Þorri," who is the Norse god of winter. During this festival, people gather to enjoy a feast featuring traditional Icelandic foods, many of which may be unfamiliar to tourists. Dishes often include hákarl (fermented shark), svið (singed sheep's head), and various types of cured meats and fish. This is a time when locals come together to embrace their cultural roots, and visitors are encouraged to partake in the festivities, often joining in for traditional songs and dances. Various towns and cities host their own Þorrablót celebrations, making it a fantastic way to experience Icelandic culture firsthand.

As spring arrives, the festival of Sumardagurinn Fyrsti (First Day of Summer) takes place in mid-April. Despite being celebrated during one of the coldest months, this festival marks the official start of summer in Iceland, according to the old calendar. It is a public holiday celebrated with parades, music, and local events throughout the country. Towns often host various activities, including traditional games, horse shows, and community picnics. This festive atmosphere brings together people of all ages, as families and friends gather to welcome the brighter days ahead. Visitors during this time will find local shops and markets filled with special summer-themed goods and treats, making it a delightful time to look around the communities.

In June, the National Day of Iceland is celebrated on the 17th, commemorating the establishment of the Republic of Iceland in 1944. This day is marked by vibrant parades, music, and cultural performances throughout the country. Reykjavík hosts one of the largest celebrations, featuring colorful floats, marching bands, and traditional dancers. The day is filled with festivities, including speeches from local leaders, games for children, and, of course, plenty of food stalls offering local delicacies. National Day is a time of pride for Icelanders, and tourists are welcomed to join in the celebrations, allowing them to witness the national spirit in full swing.

During the summer months, Reykjavík Culture Night takes place in August, a lively event that showcases the city's arts and culture scene. This festival features a wide array of activities, including art exhibitions, concerts, street performances, and guided tours. The entire city comes alive as museums and galleries open their doors for free, allowing visitors to look around Icelandic art and history. Food stalls offering local treats line the streets, and live music can be heard throughout the downtown area. The atmosphere is festive and inclusive, making it an excellent opportunity for tourists to experience the vibrant cultural fabric of Reykjavík.

As autumn approaches, Iceland celebrates Jólasveinar, or the Yule Lads, during the Christmas season. The tradition of the Yule Lads originates from old Icelandic folklore, where these mischievous figures come down from the mountains to visit children in the days leading up to Christmas. The Yule Lads are known for their playful antics and quirky personalities, and each night leading up to Christmas, one Yule Lad arrives, leaving small gifts or potatoes in children's shoes. The festive spirit is palpable throughout the country, with Christmas markets, lights, and decorations adorning towns and cities. Traditional foods, such as hangikjöt (smoked lamb) and jólasveinar (Christmas cookies), are enjoyed during this time. Various events are organized, including concerts and church services, making it a wonderful time to experience Icelandic holiday traditions.

In addition to these major festivals, Iceland also hosts a variety of local events and celebrations that reflect regional culture and heritage. For instance, the Reykjavík Jazz Festival in September attracts music lovers from around the world, showcasing local and international jazz talent. Similarly, the Iceland Airwaves music festival, held in November, brings together musicians and fans for a lively celebration of diverse music genres in venues across Reykjavík. These festivals often provide visitors with a chance to experience Iceland's contemporary arts scene while enjoying live performances in an intimate setting.

Outdoor activities are also celebrated in Iceland through various sports events, such as the Icelandic Horse World Championships held every few years, where the unique Icelandic horse is showcased in competitions and exhibitions. The emphasis on outdoor and nature-based events is a testament to the Icelandic people's connection to their environment.

For those visiting during specific times of the year, it's important to check the local calendar for any festivals or events that may be taking place. Participating in these celebrations provides an authentic glimpse into Icelandic life and customs, allowing tourists to engage with locals and gain a deeper understanding of the culture. Many towns also have their own unique festivals that celebrate local history, crafts, or foods, providing opportunities for visitors to look around areas outside of Reykjavík and find out the charm of Icelandic communities.

Traditional Festivals Celebrating Seasons

Iceland is a country with a rich tapestry of cultural traditions, many of which are tied to the changing seasons. The Icelandic calendar is marked by several traditional festivals that celebrate the unique rhythms of nature, reflecting the country's deep connection to its environment. These seasonal festivals not only showcase Icelandic heritage but also provide tourists with a wonderful opportunity to engage with the local culture and experience the beauty of the land through various celebrations.

One of the most significant seasonal festivals is Þorrablót, celebrated in midwinter, typically from late January to early March. This festival honors the Norse god Þorri and is rooted in ancient traditions that date back to the Viking Age. Þorrablót serves as a midwinter feast, bringing communities together to enjoy traditional Icelandic foods that have been preserved through centuries. During this time, people indulge in dishes such as fermented shark (hákarl), singed sheep's head (svið), and a variety of cured meats. The atmosphere is festive, with music, singing, and storytelling often accompanying the meals. This celebration allows visitors to not only taste traditional dishes but also to immerse themselves in Icelandic culture and community spirit.

As winter gives way to spring, Icelanders celebrate Sumardagurinn Fyrsti, or the First Day of Summer, which occurs in mid-April. This festival marks the official beginning of summer according to the old Icelandic calendar. Despite the chilly temperatures, this day is celebrated with enthusiasm and includes parades, music, and various community events. Towns and cities host gatherings where families can enjoy outdoor activities, games, and performances. The celebration is a reminder that brighter days are ahead, and it reflects the Icelanders' resilience in the face of challenging weather conditions. Visitors during this time can experience the joyful atmosphere and participate in local festivities, gaining insight into the seasonal customs of the Icelandic people.

In June, Icelanders celebrate National Day on the 17th, which commemorates the establishment of the Republic of Iceland in 1944. This day is marked by parades, concerts, and cultural events across the country. In Reykjavík, the capital, festivities include traditional music, dancing, and colorful floats. Families come together to celebrate with picnics, and many wear traditional Icelandic clothing, showcasing the country's rich cultural heritage. National Day is an occasion for Icelanders to express their pride in their history and independence, and visitors are warmly welcomed to join in the celebrations, enjoying the lively atmosphere and cultural displays.

As summer progresses, the Reykjavík Culture Night takes place in August, highlighting the vibrant arts scene in the capital. This annual festival showcases a variety of cultural activities, including art exhibitions, theater performances, live music, and workshops. The entire city comes alive with events spread across different venues, making it easy for tourists to look around and participate in the rich cultural offerings. Culture Night is an excellent opportunity to experience Icelandic creativity and artistic expression while enjoying the long summer evenings.

As autumn approaches, the Jólasveinar tradition begins, leading up to the Christmas season. This festive period, starting in December, centers around the 13 Yule Lads, mischievous figures from Icelandic folklore who visit children in the days leading up to Christmas. Each night, one Yule Lad arrives, bringing small gifts or potatoes for children, depending on their behavior. The period leading up to Christmas is filled with festive markets, lights, and decorations, creating a magical atmosphere throughout the country. Traditional foods are prepared and enjoyed, including smoked lamb (hangikjöt) and various baked goods. Many towns host Christmas markets where visitors can shop for local crafts and seasonal treats while enjoying the festive spirit.

Throughout the year, various regional festivals also celebrate local customs, traditions, and the changing seasons. For example, the Reykjavík Arts Festival, held in May and June, brings together local and international artists for performances in theater, music, and dance. This festival highlights the cultural vibrancy of Iceland and provides an opportunity for visitors to experience world-class performances in a beautiful setting. Similarly, the Iceland Airwaves music festival, held in November, showcases emerging and established musicians from Iceland and around the world, transforming the city into a vibrant hub of music and creativity.

In addition to these festivals, seasonal events tied to the natural world are also celebrated. Summer solstice events in June commemorate the longest day of the year, with various gatherings held to celebrate the light and the beauty of nature. Many communities host bonfires, music, and festivities to honor this time of year when the sun barely sets, creating a magical atmosphere.

Throughout the winter months, the winter solstice is also recognized, marking the shortest day of the year. This time is often celebrated with candlelight, storytelling, and community gatherings, as people come together to share warmth and hope during the darkest days.

Local Art and Music Scene

Iceland boasts a vibrant and dynamic local art and music scene that reflects the country's rich cultural heritage and the creativity of its people. The artistic expression found in Iceland is deeply influenced by its dramatic landscapes, historical roots, and the close-knit nature of its communities. For tourists, exploring Iceland's art and music offers an insightful glimpse into the heart and soul of the nation.

The Icelandic art scene has evolved significantly over the years, and it is now characterized by a mix of traditional and contemporary influences. One of the most recognizable forms of Icelandic art is painting, with many artists drawing inspiration from the stunning natural landscapes surrounding them. Artists such as Jóhannes Kjarval have played a pivotal role in defining Icelandic art. Kjarval is known for his colorful and expressive landscapes that capture the essence of the Icelandic terrain. His works often reflect the interplay of light and color found in nature, making them a favorite among locals and visitors alike.

In addition to painting, Iceland is home to a thriving craft and design scene. Many artisans specialize in traditional crafts, such as weaving, pottery, and woodworking. The use of natural materials is common, and many artisans take pride in creating functional and beautiful items that reflect Icelandic culture. Local markets and craft fairs, particularly in Reykjavík, provide tourists with the opportunity to purchase unique handmade items, ranging from woolen goods to intricate jewelry inspired by Iceland's nature.

Reykjavík, the capital city, serves as the cultural hub of Iceland, hosting numerous galleries and exhibition spaces that showcase both emerging and established artists. The Reykjavík Art Museum is one of the largest visual art institutions in Iceland, featuring a diverse collection of contemporary art and historical works. The museum often hosts temporary exhibitions, providing visitors with a chance to see the latest trends in Icelandic art. Another prominent venue is Hafnarhús, which focuses on modern and contemporary art, offering a platform for local artists to exhibit their work and engage with the community.

The music scene in Iceland is equally vibrant and diverse, with a wide range of genres and styles represented. Iceland is known for its rich musical tradition, which blends folk music with modern influences. Rímur, a form of epic poetry recitation, is a traditional Icelandic musical genre that dates back to the medieval period. While rooted in history, this tradition has influenced many contemporary Icelandic musicians who incorporate elements of folk music into their work.

One of the most internationally recognized Icelandic musicians is Björk, whose innovative and eclectic style has garnered acclaim worldwide. Björk's music often combines various genres, including pop, electronic, and classical, showcasing her unique voice and artistic vision. She is known for her visually striking performances and elaborate music videos, which further highlight her artistic approach. Alongside Björk, other popular Icelandic musicians such as Sigur Rós and Of Monsters and Men have also gained international recognition, contributing to the global appreciation of Icelandic music.

The Iceland Airwaves music festival, held annually in Reykjavík, is a key event that celebrates both local and international music. This festival showcases a wide array of genres, from indie rock to electronic music, and features performances by established artists and emerging talent. The festival draws music lovers from around the world, creating a lively atmosphere throughout the city. Many venues across Reykjavík open their doors for concerts, allowing visitors to find out new sounds while enjoying the vibrant nightlife.

In addition to music festivals, live music is a staple in Iceland's cultural landscape. Many bars and cafés in Reykjavík host live performances, showcasing local bands and musicians. These intimate venues provide a
great opportunity for tourists to experience the local music scene firsthand while mingling with residents. Many musicians in Iceland take inspiration from the natural

surroundings, and this connection is often reflected in their lyrics and melodies, adding depth to the musical experience.

The Icelandic film industry has also begun to gain recognition on the international stage, with a number of films showcasing the stunning landscapes and unique culture of the country. Filmmakers like Benedikt Erlingsson and Grímur Hákonarson have received acclaim for their works that blend storytelling with the beauty of Icelandic nature. The connection between film and the environment has led to a growing interest in cinematic tourism, where visitors are inspired to look around the locations featured in popular films shot in Iceland.

Throughout the year, various cultural events and festivals celebrate the arts in Iceland. The Reykjavík Culture Night, for instance, showcases not only music but also visual arts, literature, and culinary delights. The entire city becomes a stage for artists, musicians, and performers, transforming public spaces into vibrant galleries and concert venues. Tourists are encouraged to participate in these events, providing an excellent opportunity to experience the creativity of Icelandic artists and their works.

The Northern Lights (Aurora Borealis) also play a role in the artistic inspiration of many Icelandic artists and musicians. The natural phenomenon is celebrated in various art forms, and visitors can find artworks that depict the stunning colors and movement of the auroras. Many musicians draw inspiration from the mystical qualities of the Northern

Lights, creating compositions that capture the beauty and wonder of this natural spectacle.

Iceland's commitment to sustainability and environmental consciousness is also reflected in its art and music scene. Many artists focus on themes of nature, climate change, and conservation, using their platforms to raise awareness about environmental issues. This connection to nature not only influences their work but also encourages a dialogue about the importance of preserving Iceland's stunning landscapes for future generations.

Cultural Performances and Theater

Iceland boasts a vibrant cultural scene, particularly in the realms of performances and theater, where traditional storytelling and modern expressions converge to create a unique artistic landscape. The country's artistic heritage is deeply rooted in its history, folklore, and the dramatic natural environment that surrounds it. For tourists, experiencing the cultural performances and theatrical productions in Iceland provides a rich insight into the values, traditions, and creativity of its people.

The tradition of storytelling has always held a significant place in Icelandic culture, often linked to the country's rich history of sagas and folklore. These tales have been passed down through generations and frequently inspire contemporary theatrical performances. Many Icelandic playwrights and actors draw on these stories, weaving them into modern narratives that resonate with both locals and visitors. This connection to storytelling is evident in various forms of performance art, including puppet shows, dance, and traditional music, all of which play a role in expressing Icelandic identity.

The Icelandic National Theatre, located in Reykjavík, serves as the primary venue for many theatrical productions. This historic theater has a rich legacy, having been established in the early 20th century, and continues to host a diverse range of performances throughout the year. From classic plays to contemporary works, the theater showcases both Icelandic and international productions. Attending a performance at the National Theatre offers visitors a chance to experience the local talent and enjoy the impressive architecture of the venue itself. Many productions are performed in Icelandic, but English subtitles are often provided, making it accessible for non-Icelandic speakers to enjoy the performances.

In addition to the National Theatre, Reykjavík's cultural landscape includes smaller theaters and performance spaces that contribute to the vibrant arts scene. The Theatre of Iceland focuses on innovative and experimental productions, often exploring contemporary themes relevant to society. These smaller venues foster a sense of intimacy and allow for creative experimentation, providing audiences with unique and engaging experiences. Many of these theaters also engage in community projects and workshops, encouraging participation from locals and tourists alike.

Dance is another important aspect of Iceland's cultural performance scene. The Iceland Dance Company is the leading contemporary dance ensemble in the country, known for its dynamic performances that blend various styles and influences. The company regularly collaborates with local and international choreographers, resulting in innovative works that look around themes relevant to Icelandic life and culture. Dance performances often take place in different venues across Reykjavík and beyond, showcasing the talent and creativity of Icelandic dancers and providing an exciting experience for those who attend.

The influence of music is deeply woven into Iceland's cultural fabric, with numerous musical performances complementing theater and dance productions. Festivals celebrating music, such as the Reykjavík Arts Festival, feature interdisciplinary performances that include elements of theater, dance, and music. This festival showcases both established and emerging artists, creating a platform for creative collaboration and exploration. Visitors can experience a diverse range of genres, from classical to contemporary, and often enjoy performances in unique settings throughout the city.

For those interested in traditional music, Rímur is a form of epic poetry that has been performed in Iceland for centuries. This traditional style often features a solo singer or a group performing narratives that celebrate Icelandic history and folklore. While Rímur may not be as commonly encountered today, some cultural festivals and events continue to feature this captivating form of storytelling. Participating in such performances allows visitors to appreciate the depth of Iceland's musical heritage.

Iceland also hosts various festivals throughout the year that celebrate its rich cultural heritage. Reykjavík Culture Night is a highlight, showcasing local artists, musicians, and performers across the city. On this night, galleries, museums, and public spaces open their doors to the public, creating a vibrant atmosphere filled with music, art, and theatrical performances. Tourists can experience the spirit of community and creativity while find outing new artistic expressions.

Another significant cultural event is the Icelandic Festival of Literature, which features readings, discussions, and performances by local and international authors. This festival not only emphasizes the importance of literature in Icelandic culture but also showcases various forms of artistic expression that stem from storytelling traditions. Visitors can attend workshops, panels, and readings, gaining deeper insights into the literary landscape of Iceland.

In addition to the formal performances, the streets of Reykjavík are often alive with artistic expression, as musicians and performers showcase their talents in public spaces. The city is known for its vibrant street music scene, where local artists play everything from folk music to pop, creating a lively atmosphere that encourages passersby to stop and enjoy the music. This spontaneous form of performance adds to the overall cultural experience, making it easy for visitors to immerse themselves in the local arts scene.

For tourists eager to look around Iceland's cultural performances and theater, it's advisable to check local listings for upcoming events and productions. Many theaters and performance venues have websites and social media pages where they post information about shows, ticket prices, and schedules. Attending a live performance not only supports local artists but also provides a unique perspective on Icelandic culture that goes beyond the typical tourist experience.

Local Artisans and Crafts

Iceland is home to a vibrant community of local artisans and craftsmen whose work reflects the country's unique culture, natural resources, and artistic heritage. The craftsmanship in Iceland is deeply rooted in traditions that have been passed down through generations, and today, these artisans continue to create beautiful and functional items that capture the essence of Icelandic identity. For tourists, find outing local crafts and interacting with artisans can provide an enriching experience that connects them to Iceland's rich history and creativity.

One of the most prominent forms of Icelandic craftsmanship is woolen goods, particularly items made from Icelandic sheep wool. The Icelandic sheep is known for its unique wool, which consists of two layers: a soft inner layer and a coarse outer layer that provides excellent insulation and water resistance. Artisans skillfully use this wool to create a variety of products, including sweaters, hats, scarves, and blankets. The iconic lopapeysa, or Icelandic wool sweater, is a must-see for visitors. These sweaters are often decorated with traditional patterns that reflect the natural beauty of Iceland, such as snowflakes, mountains, and volcanic landscapes. Many artisans sell their woolen goods at local markets, craft fairs, and boutiques, offering tourists the chance to purchase high-quality, handmade items that are both practical and beautiful.

In addition to wool, pottery and ceramics are important aspects of Icelandic craft. Local potters often draw inspiration from the surrounding landscapes, creating unique pieces that reflect the colors and textures of Iceland's natural environment. Handcrafted ceramics can be found in many forms, including functional dishware, decorative pieces, and sculptures. Artisans often use traditional techniques, such as wheel throwing and hand-building, to create their works, making each piece distinct. Visiting pottery studios allows tourists to see artisans at work and gain insight into the creative process, and many studios offer workshops where visitors can try their hand at pottery-making.

Jewelry-making is another prominent craft in Iceland, with many artisans creating unique pieces that incorporate natural materials such as lava, stones, and even bits of Icelandic silver. The use of local materials allows artists to create jewelry that reflects the beauty of the Icelandic landscape. Many jewelers emphasize sustainable practices, often sourcing materials responsibly and crafting their pieces with care. Tourists can find stunning rings, necklaces, and bracelets in various styles, from contemporary designs to traditional pieces inspired by Icelandic folklore. Visiting local jewelry shops not only provides the opportunity to purchase one-of-a-kind items but also supports local artisans.

Woodworking is a craft that showcases the skills of Icelandic artisans, particularly in the creation of functional items and decorative art. Many artisans use locally sourced wood, such as birch and pine, to craft beautiful furniture, kitchen utensils, and decorative items. Some craftsmen also engage in traditional boat-building, reflecting Iceland's maritime heritage. The craftsmanship involved in woodworking is meticulous, and many artisans take pride in using age-old techniques that honor the natural materials they work with. Tourists can find woodworking shops in various towns, and some even offer workshops where visitors can learn about the craft and create their own wooden items.

Iceland's artistic community also includes glassblowers who produce stunning glass art, ranging from intricate vases to beautiful glass sculptures. These artisans often draw inspiration from the natural elements of Iceland, such as glaciers and the Northern Lights, resulting in pieces that reflect the beauty and magic of the landscape. Watching a glassblowing demonstration is a captivating experience, as artisans showcase their skills and explain the processes involved in creating their art. Many glass workshops have shops attached where visitors can purchase the finished pieces, allowing them to take home a unique reminder of their time in Iceland.

Another area of craftsmanship that has gained popularity is printmaking and textiles. Local artists create unique prints that often depict Icelandic landscapes, wildlife, and cultural motifs. These prints can be found in various forms, including posters, cards, and fabric designs. Textile artists use traditional techniques to create beautiful woven items, including rugs and tapestries, which reflect the rich colors and textures of Iceland's environment. Many artists open their studios to the public, offering workshops and demonstrations that provide visitors with an opportunity to engage with the creative process.

Throughout the year, various craft fairs and markets take place in Iceland, showcasing the talents of local artisans. Events like the Reykjavík Christmas Market and the Handcrafted Iceland Fair allow tourists to look around a wide array of handmade goods, from pottery and textiles to jewelry and food products. These markets provide a platform for artisans to connect with the community and share their crafts with visitors. Shoppers can enjoy a festive atmosphere while supporting local makers and finding unique souvenirs that capture the essence of Iceland.

For tourists interested in exploring Iceland's craft scene, visiting local galleries and studios is highly recommended. Many artisans are passionate about sharing their stories and processes, and they often welcome visitors into their workshops. This interaction offers a deeper understanding of the craftsmanship and dedication that goes into creating each piece. Additionally, many artisans sell their work online, providing the option for tourists to browse and purchase items even after returning home.

Local Crafts Workshops

Iceland is a treasure trove of local crafts and artistic traditions, with many artisans dedicated to preserving and sharing their skills. For tourists, participating in local crafts workshops offers a unique opportunity to connect with Icelandic culture while learning about traditional techniques and creating something special to take home. These workshops cater to a variety of interests, allowing visitors to look around different forms of craftsmanship, from textiles and pottery to woodworking and jewelry making. Engaging in these hands-on experiences not only deepens understanding of Iceland's artistic heritage but also provides a chance to interact with skilled artisans who are passionate about their craft.

One of the most popular types of workshops involves textile arts, particularly the creation of woolen goods. Icelandic wool is renowned for its quality, and many artisans conduct workshops where participants can learn to spin wool and weave traditional items like scarves, hats, or blankets. These workshops typically include an introduction to the different types of Icelandic sheep and their wool, along with demonstrations of spinning and weaving techniques. Participants often leave with a finished product, along with the knowledge of how to continue crafting at home. This experience not only allows tourists to create something tangible but also connects them to the traditional practices that have sustained Icelandic communities for generations.

Pottery and ceramics workshops are another fantastic option for those interested in hands-on crafting. Many local studios offer classes that cover everything from basic techniques to more advanced methods of wheel throwing and hand-building. Participants can look around their creativity by designing and crafting their own pieces, such as mugs, bowls, or decorative items. The friendly atmosphere in these workshops encourages experimentation, and participants often find themselves immersed in the process, enjoying the tactile experience of working with clay. Once their creations are fired and glazed, participants can take home a unique piece of Icelandic craftsmanship that reflects their personal style.

For those drawn to the natural beauty of Iceland, woodworking workshops provide an engaging way to create functional art. Many artisans focus on using locally sourced materials, and workshops often cover techniques such as carving, shaping, and finishing wood. Participants might have the opportunity to create items such as wooden utensils, furniture, or decorative pieces. These workshops emphasize sustainable practices and often educate participants on the importance of respecting natural resources. Learning from skilled woodworkers in a serene setting, surrounded by Iceland's stunning landscapes, adds a layer of inspiration to the crafting experience.

In addition to these traditional crafts, jewelry-making workshops are popular among visitors looking to create something personal and meaningful. Local jewelers often offer classes where participants can learn techniques such as metalworking, stone setting, and design principles. These workshops cater to all skill levels, from beginners to those with some prior experience. Participants can create their own unique pieces, such as rings or necklaces, often incorporating Icelandic materials like lava stones or silver. This connection to local materials enhances the significance of the jewelry, making it a cherished keepsake or a thoughtful gift for loved ones.

Glassblowing workshops offer a mesmerizing experience for tourists interested in this delicate art form. In these workshops, participants can learn the basics of glassblowing techniques under the guidance of skilled artisans. The process of shaping molten glass into beautiful forms is both captivating and rewarding, allowing participants to create unique glass items such as vases, ornaments, or functional pieces. Watching the transformation of glass from a molten state into a finished product provides a sense of accomplishment, and the vibrant colors and intricate designs often reflect the natural beauty of Iceland itself.

Craft workshops are widely available in Reykjavík, where many artisans open their studios to the public. However, you can also find workshops in smaller towns throughout the country, allowing tourists to engage with local culture in various settings. Many workshops welcome visitors year-round, but it's a good idea to check schedules and book in advance, especially during peak tourist seasons when classes may fill up quickly.

Additionally, some tours offer craft experiences as part of a larger itinerary, where visitors can combine sightseeing with hands-on activities. For example, a tour might include a visit to a local farm where wool products are made, followed by a workshop on spinning or weaving. This kind of immersive experience not only enhances the crafting aspect but also deepens understanding of Iceland's agricultural traditions and the connection between the land and the craftspeople.

Participating in local crafts workshops is not only enjoyable but also promotes a sense of community. Many artisans value sharing their skills and knowledge, creating a welcoming environment for participants. Tourists often leave workshops not just with a crafted item but also with stories, friendships, and a deeper appreciation for the traditions that shape Icelandic culture.

Local Fashion and Dress Codes

Iceland's fashion and dress codes are shaped by its unique climate, geography, and cultural heritage. For tourists, understanding the local fashion scene can enhance their experience while visiting, allowing them to blend in with the locals and appreciate the country's artistic expressions through clothing. Icelandic fashion is a blend of practicality and creativity, reflecting the nation's lifestyle and the influence of its stunning landscapes.

The weather in Iceland can be unpredictable, with rapid changes that require versatile clothing choices. As a result, layering is a common practice among locals. The typical Icelandic wardrobe consists of several layers that can be added or removed depending on the weather conditions. Base layers made of wool or thermal materials are essential, providing warmth and comfort. Icelandic wool is particularly favored due to its natural insulating properties, moisture-wicking abilities, and breathability. A popular item is the lopapeysa, the traditional Icelandic wool sweater, characterized by its unique circular yoke pattern. These sweaters are not only functional but also stylish, often worn casually or dressed up for various occasions.

Outer layers are crucial for protecting against the elements. Waterproof and windproof jackets are a must, as Icelandic weather can bring rain and strong winds at any time of year. Locals often opt for practical yet fashionable outdoor wear that allows them to enjoy outdoor activities comfortably. Additionally, sturdy footwear is essential, especially for those planning to look around the country's rugged terrain. Waterproof hiking boots are recommended for adventures in the beautiful landscapes, while more casual options like stylish sneakers are also common in urban areas.

In urban settings, particularly in Reykjavík, the fashion scene is more eclectic and reflects global trends while maintaining a distinctly Icelandic twist. The city is home to a vibrant community of designers and boutiques that showcase local talent. Many Icelandic designers incorporate traditional materials and techniques into modern designs, creating unique pieces that celebrate their cultural heritage. Tourists can find everything from contemporary streetwear to elegant dresses made from high-quality fabrics. The emphasis on sustainable fashion is also growing, with several brands focusing on eco-friendly materials and production methods, reflecting a wider awareness of environmental issues.

Accessories play a significant role in Icelandic fashion, with locals often using them to express their individuality. Scarves, hats, and gloves made from Icelandic wool are not only practical but also serve as stylish accents to an outfit. Handmade jewelry, particularly pieces that incorporate natural elements such as stones and wood, are popular among both locals and visitors. These accessories can often be found at craft fairs and local shops, providing a meaningful way to connect with Icelandic craftsmanship.

When it comes to special occasions, such as weddings or cultural events, traditional attire may be worn. The lopapeysa remains a popular choice, but during significant celebrations, locals may also wear national costumes. The Icelandic national dress, known as Þjóðbúningur, consists of intricate, hand-stitched garments often adorned with beautiful patterns and embroidery. While this traditional attire is typically reserved for special occasions, its significance in Icelandic culture remains strong.

While exploring Iceland, tourists should be mindful of local customs related to dress codes. Generally, Icelanders have a relaxed attitude toward clothing, valuing comfort and practicality. However, when visiting religious sites or attending formal events, dressing modestly is advised. In more rural areas, visitors may notice that locals tend to dress more conservatively, particularly in traditional communities.

The influence of the Icelandic climate on fashion is not only about practicality but also about style. Fashion in Iceland embraces individuality, with many locals choosing to express themselves through their clothing choices. This creativity is often reflected in how people mix and match different styles, patterns, and colors, creating outfits that are both functional and expressive. Tourists will find that locals appreciate effort in personal style, whether it's through a unique accessory or a carefully chosen outfit.

When it comes to shopping for fashion in Iceland, Reykjavík is the hub of local designers and boutiques. Popular shopping areas like Laugavegur street are lined with shops offering a mix of traditional and contemporary Icelandic fashion. Tourists can find unique pieces that celebrate Icelandic culture, from clothing to accessories and home goods. Additionally, several annual craft fairs, such as the Reykjavík Design March, showcase local designers, offering visitors a chance to find out and purchase one-of-a-kind items directly from the makers.

Icelandic fashion and dress codes are influenced by the country's climate, culture, and artistic expression. The practical need for warmth and protection against the elements is balanced with a growing emphasis on individuality and style. Tourists can immerse themselves in this vibrant scene by embracing the local customs, exploring artisan shops, and participating in workshops that highlight traditional crafts.

CHAPTER 10

PLACES TO VISIT

Free Tourist Attractions

Iceland is a country renowned for its stunning natural beauty and rich cultural heritage, offering a plethora of attractions that are not only breathtaking but also free to visit. For tourists exploring this remarkable land, taking advantage of these free tourist attractions can enhance their experience without straining their budget.

One of the most iconic free attractions in Iceland is the Golden Circle, a popular tourist route that encompasses some of the country's most remarkable natural wonders. The first stop along this route is Þingvellir National Park, a UNESCO World Heritage Site where visitors can witness the dramatic rift between the North American and Eurasian tectonic plates. This geological wonder not only offers stunning views but also has significant historical importance as the site of Iceland's first parliament, established in 930 AD. Visitors can look around the park's hiking trails, take in the breathtaking scenery, and even walk between the tectonic plates, making it a truly memorable experience.

Another highlight of the Golden Circle is Geysir Geothermal Area, home to the famous Strokkur geyser, which erupts every few minutes, shooting hot water high into the air.

While some areas may have entrance fees for specific attractions, the geothermal area itself is free to look around. Tourists can wander through the bubbling hot springs, steaming vents, and colorful mineral deposits, marveling at the power of geothermal activity in this unique landscape. It's an excellent spot for photography and understanding the forces that shape Iceland's natural environment.

Nearby, the Gullfoss waterfall offers a spectacular display of nature's power. This magnificent waterfall cascades into a rugged canyon, creating a stunning sight that draws visitors year-round. The path leading to the viewing platforms is well-maintained and free to access, allowing guests to experience the awe-inspiring beauty of Gullfoss up close. Whether in summer, when the surrounding area is green and green, or in winter, when ice and snow create a magical scene, Gullfoss is a must-see attraction that showcases Iceland's natural grandeur.

For those interested in Iceland's cultural heritage, a visit to Reykjavík provides numerous free attractions. The city's central area is home to Hallgrímskirkja, a striking church that dominates the skyline. While there is a small fee to go up the tower for a panoramic view of the city, visitors can still enjoy the church's unique architecture and beautiful surroundings without spending a dime. The church is an excellent example of modern Icelandic design, inspired by the natural columns of basalt rock found throughout the country.

In addition to Hallgrímskirkja, the Harpa Concert Hall is another architectural marvel worth visiting. This stunning building, located by the harbor, features a striking glass facade that reflects the light in various colors, creating an ever-changing spectacle. Harpa often hosts free concerts and events, so checking the schedule may lead to an enjoyable cultural experience. The surrounding area also offers picturesque views of the waterfront and nearby mountains, making it a great spot to relax and take in the scenery.

For nature enthusiasts, Reykjavík's local parks and waterfront areas provide ample opportunities for outdoor activities at no cost. Elliðaárdalur Valley is a beautiful park located just a short distance from the city center, offering walking and cycling paths along the river, as well as green greenery and wildlife. It's a peaceful escape where visitors can enjoy a leisurely stroll or a picnic while observing the local flora and fauna.

Another stunning natural attraction is Sólheimasandur, the site of the famous US Navy plane wreck. The wreckage of the Douglas DC-3 airplane, which crashed on the black sand beach in 1973, has become a popular photo spot. While it requires a hike of approximately four miles from the nearest parking area to reach the site, the trek offers a chance to experience the desolate beauty of Iceland's landscapes. The stark contrast of the white wreck against the black sand is a striking sight and makes for a unique photographic opportunity.

Iceland's incredible landscapes also include numerous waterfalls, many of which are accessible for free. Some notable examples include Seljalandsfoss and Skógafoss, both located along the South Coast. Seljalandsfoss is particularly special because visitors can walk behind the waterfall, providing a unique perspective and a memorable experience. Skógafoss, with its powerful flow and expansive width, creates a breathtaking sight, often accompanied by rainbows on sunny days. These natural wonders highlight the dramatic beauty of Iceland and are easily accessible for those looking to look around the outdoors.

As for historical sites, Reykjavík's National Museum of Iceland offers free admission on certain days, allowing tourists to delve into the country's rich history. The museum's exhibitions cover everything from the Viking Age to modern Icelandic culture, providing valuable insights into the nation's heritage. Even when entrance fees apply, many outdoor historical sites, such as the Árbær Open Air Museum, offer a glimpse into Iceland's past without breaking the bank. Iceland is also famous for its hot springs, many of which are free or have minimal entrance fees. While popular locations like the Blue Lagoon charge for access, there are several natural hot springs scattered throughout the country where visitors can relax in warm, mineral-rich waters without spending much. Places like Reykjadalur near Hveragerði offer a scenic hike followed by a soak in the hot river, creating a delightful outdoor experience that immerses visitors in Iceland's geothermal wonders.

For those traveling with a keen interest in wildlife, Iceland's diverse ecosystems provide opportunities for free wildlife watching. Migratory birds, including puffins, can be observed along the coasts during the summer months, with several accessible birdwatching locations. Tourists may also spot seals and whales from various points along the coast, and while boat tours typically charge fees, many areas allow for shore-based wildlife observation without cost.

Iceland is filled with a multitude of free tourist attractions that showcase the country's stunning natural beauty, rich cultural heritage, and vibrant community spirit. From the breathtaking landscapes of the Golden Circle to the unique experiences in Reykjavík, visitors can find countless opportunities to look around without spending a fortune.

Paid Tourist Attractions

Iceland is a country filled with breathtaking landscapes and rich cultural experiences, many of which come with entrance fees that help maintain these sites and support the local economy. For tourists, understanding the paid attractions can enhance their visit, providing opportunities to look around unique aspects of Iceland's natural beauty, history, and cultural heritage. These attractions often offer guided experiences, educational opportunities, and amenities that add significant value to the visit.

One of the most famous paid attractions in Iceland is the Blue Lagoon, a geothermal spa located in a lava field near Grindavík. The Blue Lagoon is known for its milky blue waters, rich in minerals like silica and sulfur, which are said to have healing properties. Visitors can enjoy soaking in the warm water while surrounded by stunning volcanic landscapes. The facility offers various services, including spa treatments, massages, and a restaurant serving local cuisine. Tickets can be purchased online in advance, as the Blue Lagoon can get quite busy, especially during peak tourist seasons. Visiting the Blue Lagoon provides a luxurious and relaxing experience, making it a popular stop for those traveling to or from the airport.

Another notable paid attraction is the Golden Circle, a popular tourist route that includes several key sites, many of which charge for entrance. The first major stop is Þingvellir National Park, a UNESCO World Heritage Site where visitors can learn about the history of Iceland's parliament and see the rift between the North American and Eurasian tectonic plates. While entrance to the park is free, certain activities and facilities, such as the visitor center, may have fees. The nearby Geysir Geothermal Area features the famous Strokkur geyser, which erupts every few minutes. This natural wonder can be enjoyed at no cost, but nearby guided tours that provide deeper insights into the geothermal features may require a fee. Lastly, the impressive Gullfoss waterfall is part of the Golden Circle; access to the waterfall itself is free, but parking may come with a small fee.

The South Coast of Iceland is another region filled with paid attractions that showcase the country's natural wonders. One of the most popular sites is the Seljalandsfoss waterfall, which is famous for the unique opportunity it offers visitors to walk behind the falls. While the waterfall is free to visit, there is a parking fee. Nearby, Skógafoss, another stunning waterfall, charges a small fee for parking as well, but the majestic sight of the water cascading from the cliff is well worth it. For those interested in exploring Iceland's glaciers, Sólheimajökull offers guided glacier walks, which are a paid experience but provide an unforgettable adventure on the ice.

For tourists eager to learn about Iceland's rich history and culture, several paid museums and cultural attractions are well worth a visit. The National Museum of Iceland in Reykjavík showcases the country's history from the Viking Age to modern times. The museum offers a comprehensive look at Icelandic culture through artifacts, photographs, and interactive exhibits. Admission fees support the museum's operations and educational programs. Another important cultural site is the Reykjavík Art Museum, which encompasses several locations, including Hafnarhús, Kjarvalsstaðir, and Ásmundarsafn, showcasing contemporary Icelandic art as well as international exhibitions. Admission fees vary, but the museum often hosts special events and temporary exhibitions, providing diverse cultural experiences.

For those interested in the natural sciences, the Whales of Iceland exhibition is a unique paid attraction located in Reykjavík. This interactive exhibition features life-sized models of various whale species found in Icelandic waters. Visitors can learn about the marine environment, whale biology, and conservation efforts. The experience often includes guided tours and educational presentations, making it an enriching experience for all ages.

Iceland is also known for its stunning natural phenomena, and many attractions charge for guided tours that provide a closer look at these wonders. The Northern Lights (Aurora Borealis) tours, for example, offer visitors the chance to see this spectacular light display during winter months. Many companies provide guided tours that take tourists to prime viewing locations, often including transportation and warm clothing. While the natural phenomenon itself is free to observe, the guided tours enhance the experience with local knowledge and expertise.

Another adventure worth paying for is a cave tour, such as the Raufarhólshellir Lava Tunnel. This fascinating underground tunnel formed by volcanic activity offers a glimpse into Iceland's geological past. Guided tours through the cave look around its unique formations, and visitors can learn about the history of the area. The fee for these tours supports the maintenance of the site and the provision of safety equipment, such as helmets and flashlights.

For tourists interested in outdoor adventures, many activities come with fees, such as glacier hiking, ice climbing, or snowmobiling on glaciers like Vatnajökull. These excursions are often led by experienced guides who ensure safety while providing insights into the stunning landscapes. While these experiences may be pricier, they offer unforgettable memories and a unique way to look around Iceland's natural beauty.

Iceland also hosts several festivals and events throughout the year, many of which charge admission fees. For instance, the Iceland Airwaves music festival showcases both local and international artists, providing a platform for diverse musical genres. Attending this festival allows visitors to immerse themselves in the vibrant music scene while experiencing the lively atmosphere of Reykjavík. Similarly, the Reykjavík Culture Night features various performances and exhibitions, and while many events are free, some workshops and performances may require tickets.

While Iceland is known for its natural attractions, the paid tourist sites offer valuable experiences that enhance a visitor's understanding of the country's culture and environment. Many of these attractions are well-maintained, providing high-quality experiences that cater to different interests, whether they are related to nature, history, or the arts.

For tourists, it is advisable to check the official websites of these attractions for the latest information on ticket prices, hours of operation, and any special events or promotions. Purchasing tickets in advance can also help avoid long lines, especially during peak tourist seasons. By exploring paid attractions alongside free ones, visitors can create a well-rounded itinerary that captures the essence of Iceland's beauty and culture.

Iceland is a country rich in history, culture, and natural beauty, and its museums play a vital role in showcasing these elements. For tourists, exploring museums offers a unique opportunity to delve into Iceland's past, appreciate its artistic expressions, and understand its contemporary society. The variety of museums across the country caters to different interests, from art and history to science and nature, providing valuable insights into what makes Iceland a distinctive destination.

One of the most prominent museums in Iceland is the National Museum of Iceland, located in Reykjavík. This museum serves as a comprehensive repository of Icelandic history and culture, featuring artifacts that date back to the Viking Age and beyond. Visitors can look around exhibitions that illustrate the country's development, including displays on early settlers, daily life, and significant historical events. The museum's collection includes textiles, tools, and even examples of ancient manuscripts, providing a tangible connection to Iceland's rich heritage. Interactive displays and informative guides enhance the experience, making it accessible and engaging for visitors of all ages. The museum also hosts temporary exhibitions that highlight specific aspects of Icelandic culture, allowing for a dynamic exploration of the nation's identity.

Another must-visit museum in Reykjavík is the Reykjavík Art Museum, which consists of three locations: Hafnarhús, Kjarvalsstaðir, and Ásmundarsafn. This museum is dedicated to contemporary Icelandic art and includes works by both established and emerging artists. Hafnarhús, located by the harbor, often features exhibitions that showcase diverse artistic expressions, including painting, sculpture, and multimedia installations. Kjarvalsstaðir is named after the famous Icelandic painter Jóhannes S. Kjarval, and it primarily focuses on his work along with other significant Icelandic artists. Ásmundarsafn is dedicated to the sculptor Ásmundur Sveinsson, housing his remarkable sculptures and artworks. The museum's emphasis on contemporary art provides visitors with a deeper understanding of the current Icelandic art scene and its influences.

For those interested in maritime history, the Icelandic Maritime Museum is an essential stop. Located in Reykjavík's old harbor, this museum tells the story of Iceland's deep connection to the sea. The exhibitions cover various aspects of maritime life, including fishing, shipbuilding, and naval history. Visitors can view historical fishing vessels, learn about traditional fishing methods, and look around the development of Iceland's maritime industry over the years. The museum often features interactive displays, making it an engaging experience for families and individuals alike.

Another fascinating museum is the Whales of Iceland exhibition, also situated in Reykjavík. This unique attraction focuses on the diverse marine life found in Icelandic waters, particularly whales. The exhibition features life-sized models of various whale species, providing visitors with a visual understanding of these magnificent creatures. Interactive displays educate guests about whale biology, migration patterns, and conservation efforts. This museum is not only informative but also highlights the importance of preserving marine ecosystems and understanding the relationship between humans and wildlife.

For those seeking a deeper dive into Iceland's cultural history, the Árbær Open Air Museum offers a unique experience. This living history museum showcases Icelandic life from the 19th century through to the 20th century, featuring relocated and restored buildings that represent different periods and styles. Visitors can walk through the village, interact with exhibits, and see traditional crafts in action. The museum hosts various events throughout the year, including festivals that celebrate traditional Icelandic culture, providing tourists with a lively and immersive experience.

Outside of Reykjavík, several museums across the country provide insights into local culture and history. The Skógar Museum, located near Skógafoss waterfall, is a comprehensive folk museum that showcases artifacts from Iceland's past, including traditional clothing, tools, and agricultural equipment. The museum also features a section dedicated to transportation history, with a collection of old cars and farm machinery. Visitors can look around the exhibits at their own pace, enjoying the extensive collection that illustrates Iceland's rural heritage.

In the Westfjords region, the Folk Museum of Iceland in Þingeyri offers a glimpse into the local history and culture of the area. This museum focuses on traditional lifestyles, featuring exhibits on fishing, farming, and daily life in the

Westfjords. The museum often organizes events that highlight local crafts, making it a great spot to learn about the region's unique practices and customs.

For art enthusiasts, the Gerðarsafn Museum in Kópavogur is an excellent destination. This museum is dedicated to the works of Icelandic painter and sculptor Gerður Helgadóttir, showcasing her contributions to modern art in Iceland. The museum often hosts temporary exhibitions featuring contemporary artists, providing a platform for artistic dialogue and innovation.

Visitors to Iceland should also consider exploring smaller, specialized museums that focus on specific aspects of Icelandic culture and history. The Icelandic Punk Museum in Reykjavík offers a unique perspective on the punk rock movement that emerged in the country during the 1980s. This museum celebrates the music, art, and culture of the punk scene, featuring memorabilia, photographs, and interviews with key figures from the movement. It's a quirky and engaging spot for those interested in contemporary Icelandic history.

In addition to traditional museums, Iceland hosts a variety of art galleries that showcase the works of local artists. These galleries often feature rotating exhibitions, providing visitors with opportunities to find out new talents and appreciate the creativity present in Iceland. Many galleries also sell artworks, allowing tourists to take home a piece of Icelandic culture.

While exploring museums, tourists are encouraged to check for special events, workshops, and guided tours. Many museums offer educational programs that can enhance the visitor experience, providing deeper insights into specific topics or techniques. Additionally, some museums have partnerships with local artists and artisans, organizing demonstrations that showcase traditional crafts.

Historical Landmarks and Monuments

Iceland is home to a rich collection of historical landmarks and monuments that offer a deep insight into its unique history, culture, and natural landscape. These sites are not just significant for their beauty or grandeur, but for the stories they carry and the role they have played in shaping the nation's identity. Exploring these landmarks provides tourists with an opportunity to connect with Iceland's past and understand the influences that have shaped its present.

One of the most important historical landmarks in Iceland is Þingvellir National Park. Located about 40 kilometers northeast of Reykjavík, Þingvellir is a UNESCO World Heritage Site and holds great historical and cultural significance. It was here, in 930 AD, that the Alþingi, Iceland's first national parliament, was established, making it one of the oldest parliaments in the world. For nearly 900 years, Þingvellir served as the heart of political and social life in Iceland. This site is not only rich in history but also holds immense geological importance as it lies in the rift valley between the Eurasian and North American tectonic plates. Visitors to Þingvellir can walk through the Almannagjá gorge, where they are literally walking between two continents, and look around the remnants of ancient gatherings. It's a place where the natural beauty of Iceland blends seamlessly with the profound significance of its history.

Another key historical landmark is Skálholt, one of the most important religious and cultural centers in Iceland for centuries. Located in southern Iceland, Skálholt was the seat of Iceland's bishops from the 11th century until the late 18th century. The site was a hub for education, religion, and administration, and it played a central role in Iceland's development during the Middle Ages. Today, visitors can look around the church at Skálholt, which is built on the site of several earlier churches. Beneath the current building are excavations that reveal the foundations of older structures, offering a glimpse into Iceland's religious history. The church grounds are surrounded by peaceful countryside, making Skálholt a serene yet historically rich destination.

The Reykholt Historic Site in West Iceland is another significant landmark, closely tied to the life of the famous Icelandic historian, poet, and politician Snorri Sturluson. Snorri lived in Reykholt during the 13th century, and his writings, including the Prose Edda and Heimskringla, are some of the most important sources of Norse mythology and Icelandic history. At Reykholt, visitors can see the ruins of Snorri's homestead, including Snorralaug, a geothermal pool that Snorri is believed to have used. There is also a museum dedicated to his life and works, providing an educational experience about one of Iceland's most influential historical figures.

The Hallgrímskirkja Church in Reykjavík, while a relatively modern construction, has become one of Iceland's most iconic landmarks. The church is named after the Icelandic poet and clergyman Hallgrímur Pétursson, who is best known for his hymns, "Passíusálmar" (The Passion Hymns). Standing at 74.5 meters tall, the church's tower is one of the tallest structures in Iceland, offering visitors panoramic views of the city and surrounding landscapes. The church's design, inspired by the basalt columns found in Iceland's volcanic landscapes, is both striking and symbolic of the nation's connection to its natural environment. Hallgrímskirkja serves as a powerful representation of Icelandic architecture, religion, and culture, making it a must-visit for tourists interested in the country's modern landmarks.

In the realm of medieval history, Hólar in Hjaltadalur is one of Iceland's most historic sites. Located in the north, Hólar was a bishopric from 1106 to 1798 and was a significant center for education and religion. Today, Hólar continues to be a place of learning, housing a small university that focuses on equine science, aquaculture, and rural tourism. Visitors can look around the old cathedral, Hóladómkirkja, which is the oldest stone church in Iceland, dating back to the 18th century. The church's historical significance, along with its beautiful architecture, makes it an important stop for those interested in Iceland's ecclesiastical history.

For those fascinated by Iceland's Viking past, the Viking World Museum in Reykjanesbær offers an engaging look into the lives of the early Norse settlers. The museum's highlight is the Íslendingur, a replica of a Viking ship that sailed from Iceland to North America in 2000 to commemorate Leif Erikson's voyage 1,000 years earlier. Visitors can learn about the Viking Age, the seafaring abilities of the Norse, and their influence on Icelandic culture. The museum not only provides historical context but also brings to life the adventurous spirit of the Vikings, making it a captivating experience for tourists.

In terms of modern history, the Höfði House in Reykjavík is another landmark of great significance. This white, wooden building is famous for being the location of the 1986 Reykjavík Summit between U.S. President Ronald Reagan and Soviet Premier Mikhail Gorbachev. This historic meeting is often credited with helping to end the Cold War. Today, Höfði House stands as a monument to diplomacy and peace, and while it is not open to the public, visitors can view the building from the outside and learn about its historical importance.

The War and Peace Museum in Hvalfjörður is dedicated to Iceland's role during World War II. The museum displays artifacts and exhibits that highlight Iceland's strategic importance during the war and its impact on the local population. Visitors can learn about the British and American occupation of Iceland, the construction of the naval base at Hvalfjörður, and the country's experience during the global conflict. The museum offers a unique perspective on Iceland's modern history, often overlooked by tourists but deeply impactful for the nation's development in the 20th century.

Iceland's rich cultural and natural heritage has earned it recognition from UNESCO, with several sites designated as World Heritage Sites, as well as others being part of the UNESCO Global Geoparks program. These recognitions are not just symbols of Iceland's unique contribution to the world's cultural and natural heritage, but also offer tourists a deeper understanding of the significance and preservation of these landscapes, cultural practices, and historical sites.

One of the most prominent UNESCO World Heritage Sites in Iceland is Þingvellir National Park. Located about 40 kilometers northeast of Reykjavík, Þingvellir holds a special place in both the history and geology of Iceland. This site is globally significant because it was the location of the Alþingi, Iceland's national parliament, which was established in 930 AD and is one of the oldest continuous parliamentary institutions in the world. For nearly 900 years, Þingvellir was where Icelanders would gather for their legislative assembly, making it a vital part of Iceland's political history. Beyond its political significance, Þingvellir is also a geological wonder. It is located in a rift valley formed by the separation of the North American and Eurasian tectonic plates. Visitors to the park can walk along the fissures in the earth, quite literally standing between two continents, and look around the stunning landscapes that are marked by waterfalls, lava fields, and crystal-clear springs. The cultural and geological importance of Þingvellir earned it a place on the UNESCO World Heritage List in 2004. As a UNESCO site, the park is protected and maintained to preserve both its historical value and its remarkable natural beauty.

Another UNESCO-recognized site in Iceland is Surtsey, an island that was created by a volcanic eruption between 1963 and 1967 off the southern coast of Iceland. Surtsey is one of the youngest islands in the world and has been left untouched by humans to allow scientists to study how life colonizes new land. The eruption that formed Surtsey began under the sea and eventually broke through the ocean surface, creating an island that has since become a natural laboratory for studying the process of ecological succession. Access to Surtsey is highly restricted to ensure that it remains a pristine environment for scientific research, but its designation as a UNESCO World Heritage Site in 2008 underscores its global importance as a place of natural and scientific significance. While tourists cannot visit Surtsey, the island's story and the ongoing research conducted there highlight the powerful forces of nature that are constantly shaping Iceland's landscape.

In addition to these two UNESCO World Heritage Sites, Iceland is home to several other notable heritage sites that, while not yet on the UNESCO list, are of significant cultural and historical importance. These include the Vatnajökull National Park, which encompasses Europe's largest glacier and a vast volcanic landscape. This park offers visitors the chance to look around some of Iceland's most dramatic natural wonders, including the Vatnajökull glacier itself, which covers over 8% of the country's land area, as well as active volcanoes, geothermal areas, and beautiful river systems. Although not officially listed as a World Heritage Site, the park has been proposed for UNESCO status due to its unique geological features and its importance to Iceland's ecosystem.

Reykholt, the historic home of the medieval writer and scholar Snorri Sturluson, is another significant heritage site in Iceland. Snorri was one of the most influential figures of his time, and his writings, such as the Prose Edda and Heimskringla, are crucial sources of Norse mythology and early Scandinavian history. Reykholt was an important cultural center during the medieval period, and today, visitors can look around Snorri's home and a museum dedicated to his life and work. While Reykholt is not a UNESCO World Heritage Site, its cultural significance is widely recognized, and it continues to be a place of pilgrimage for those interested in Icelandic history and literature.

In recent years, Iceland's natural wonders have also been recognized by UNESCO through the UNESCO Global Geoparks program, which highlights areas of international geological significance. Katla Geopark, located in the south of Iceland, is one such area. This geopark is named after the active Katla volcano and covers a region that includes glaciers, black sand beaches, and volcanic landscapes. The area has been shaped by volcanic activity and glacial movements over thousands of years, creating a stunning and diverse environment. Katla Geopark is not only geologically important but also culturally significant, as it is home to several historic sites, including ancient farms and churches.

Visitors to Katla Geopark can look around its many natural attractions, such as the Reynisfjara black sand beach and the Skógafoss waterfall, while learning about the powerful geological forces that have shaped the region.

Another important UNESCO-recognized area is the Westfjords Geopark, which was added to the UNESCO Global Geoparks network for its unique geological and cultural landscapes. This remote and rugged region in northwest Iceland is characterized by its steep cliffs, deep fjords, and glacial valleys. The Westfjords are one of the least populated areas of Iceland, and their isolation has helped preserve traditional ways of life and untouched natural environments. Tourists visiting the Westfjords can experience its incredible beauty and look around its cultural heritage, including historical fishing villages, ancient turf houses, and the folklore that is deeply embedded in the local communities.

In addition to these designated and proposed UNESCO sites, Iceland is filled with other important cultural and natural landmarks that contribute to its heritage. The Árbær Open Air Museum in Reykjavík is a living history museum that showcases traditional Icelandic homes, farms, and workshops from various periods in Iceland's history. The museum offers visitors a glimpse into daily life in Iceland in centuries past, with exhibits and events that highlight traditional crafts, farming techniques, and local customs. The preservation of these historical structures is vital to understanding the cultural evolution of Iceland and provides an accessible way for tourists to connect with the past.

The ongoing efforts to preserve and protect Iceland's heritage, whether through UNESCO designation or national initiatives, highlight the importance of these sites not only to Iceland but to the world. These landmarks and natural wonders represent key aspects of the Earth's history and human civilization, and they offer invaluable opportunities for scientific research, education, and tourism. For visitors to Iceland, these heritage sites provide a way to engage deeply with the country's cultural and natural identity, offering experiences that go beyond the surface and into the very heart of what makes Iceland so special.

Tourists visiting these sites are encouraged to respect the fragile environments and cultural significance of these places. Sustainable and responsible tourism practices are essential to ensuring that these sites remain intact for future generations to appreciate. By visiting these UNESCO-listed and other heritage sites, tourists not only enrich their travel experience but also contribute to the preservation of Iceland's most treasured landmarks.

Self-Guided Tours and Walks

Iceland is a country of extraordinary natural beauty and rich cultural history, and one of the best ways to experience it is through self-guided tours and walks. For tourists who prefer to look around at their own pace, self-guided tours offer the freedom to immerse themselves in Iceland's landscapes and history without the constraints of a formal guide or itinerary. This approach allows travelers to spend as much time as they like at each location, soaking in the experience and following their own interests. With the right preparation, self-guided tours in Iceland can be as rewarding as any organized tour, providing an in-depth look at the country's most stunning attractions.

One of the most accessible and rewarding self-guided tours in Iceland is the Golden Circle route, which covers a trio of the country's most popular and important natural attractions. The Golden Circle includes Þingvellir National Park, Geysir Geothermal Area, and Gullfoss Waterfall. These three sites are located relatively close to Reykjavík, making them a perfect option for a day trip by car. Þingvellir, as mentioned, is a UNESCO World Heritage Site and the location of Iceland's first parliament, as well as a geological marvel where the North American and Eurasian tectonic plates meet. Geysir, though not always active, is still a fascinating geothermal area with its Strokkur geyser erupting every few minutes. Nearby, Gullfoss is one of the most powerful and beautiful waterfalls in Iceland, with its cascading waters making for breathtaking views. Self-guided visitors can look around these sites in any order and spend as much time as they like at each one, reading the informational plaques, hiking the surrounding areas, and taking in the natural beauty. Many downloadable maps and apps are available that offer information about the sites, helping travelers find your way and learn about the significance of each location.

For those interested in Iceland's rich volcanic history, the Reykjanes Peninsula offers an excellent self-guided tour. This area, located southwest of Reykjavík, is filled with geothermal wonders, lava fields, and dramatic coastal landscapes. The Bridge Between Continents is one highlight, where visitors can cross a small bridge that spans the gap between the Eurasian and North American tectonic plates. The area also includes the Kleifarvatn Lake, surrounded by volcanic landscapes, and the Krysuvik Geothermal Area, where visitors can see bubbling mud pots and steam vents. The peninsula is also home to the Blue Lagoon, one of Iceland's most famous geothermal spas, which makes for a great stop to relax after a day of exploring. Self-guided visitors can easily find your way the peninsula by car, stopping at various viewpoints and attractions along the way. The region's geothermal and volcanic features are well-marked, and many locations have walking paths that allow visitors to get up close to these natural wonders.

Another incredible self-guided tour opportunity in Iceland is a visit to the South Coast, which is home to some of the country's most famous waterfalls, black sand beaches, and glacier views. A popular route for self-guided travelers starts from Reykjavík and follows Route 1 (the Ring Road) along the coast, passing through several key attractions. One of the first major stops is Seljalandsfoss, a stunning waterfall where visitors can walk behind the cascading water for a unique perspective. A short distance away is Skógafoss, another impressive waterfall that is much wider and more powerful. Farther along the route is the village of Vík, known for its black sand beach and towering sea stacks. Reynisfjara Beach is a must-see for its striking basalt columns and dramatic waves, though caution is advised as the currents can be strong. Continuing along the South Coast, visitors can also look around Sólheimajökull Glacier, which can be accessed with or without a guide for those experienced with glacier hiking. The South Coast offers plenty of options for self-guided walks and hikes, with well-marked trails and numerous points of interest.

For a more remote and rugged experience, the Snæfellsnes Peninsula in West Iceland is often described as a microcosm of the country because it contains many of the landscapes Iceland is famous for, all within a relatively small area. The peninsula is home to Snæfellsjökull National Park, which is centered around the Snæfellsjökull glacier and volcano, made famous by Jules Verne's novel *Trip to the Center of the Earth*. Visitors can drive around the peninsula, stopping at various sites such as the Búðir black church, the Lóndrangar basalt cliffs, and Kirkjufell Mountain, which is often called the most photographed mountain in Iceland. The peninsula also offers several hiking opportunities, including trails that lead to coastal viewpoints, hidden waterfalls, and lava fields. Snæfellsnes is a perfect destination for those looking for a self-guided tour that combines Iceland's natural beauty with historical and cultural landmarks.

If walking tours are more appealing, Reykjavík itself is a great city to look around on foot. The compact city center is filled with historical buildings, museums, shops, and cafes, all within easy walking distance of one another. A self-guided walking tour of Reykjavík can include stops at Hallgrímskirkja, the city's iconic church with its towering spire; Harpa Concert Hall, a modern architectural masterpiece; and the Sun Voyager sculpture by the waterfront. Visitors can also look around the Old Harbor area, where they can see fishing boats and whale-watching vessels. Reykjavík's street art scene is vibrant, and many murals and public art installations can be found throughout the city. Several apps and online guides are available that map out walking routes in Reykjavík, highlighting points of interest and providing historical information along the way.

For nature lovers, Iceland offers an abundance of hiking trails that are perfect for self-guided exploration. The Laugavegur Trail is one of the most famous hiking routes in the country, taking hikers through some of the most varied and dramatic landscapes in Iceland. The trail stretches from Landmannalaugar, known for its colorful rhyolite mountains and geothermal hot springs, to Þórsmörk, a green valley surrounded by glaciers and volcanoes. The trail typically takes four to six days to complete, and while some hikers choose to go with guided tours, many opt to hike it on their own, staying in mountain huts or camping along the way. The trail is well-marked, and there are several information points along the route to help self-guided hikers stay on track and learn about the landscapes they are passing through.

Another excellent self-guided hiking option is the Fimmvörðuháls Trail, which connects Skógafoss to Þórsmörk. This challenging but rewarding hike takes visitors through stunning landscapes, including volcanic craters formed by the 2010 eruption of Eyjafjallajökull. The trail offers breathtaking views of glaciers, waterfalls, and rugged valleys, making it one of the most scenic hikes in Iceland. Self-guided hikers should be prepared for changing weather conditions and challenging terrain, but the experience is truly unforgettable for those looking to immerse themselves in Iceland's wilderness.

Iceland's Westfjords region, though more remote, is also an excellent destination for self-guided tours and walks. This region is less visited than other parts of Iceland, but it offers some of the most dramatic and untouched landscapes in the country. Visitors can drive along the fjords, stopping at viewpoints and small villages along the way. One of the highlights of the Westfjords is Dynjandi, a magnificent waterfall that cascades down a mountainside in several tiers. A short hiking trail leads from the parking area to the base of the waterfall, offering stunning views along the way. The Westfjords are also home to some of Iceland's best birdwatching spots, including Látrabjarg, a towering cliff that is home to thousands of seabirds, including puffins.

For those looking to combine hiking with a bit of history, a visit to Reykholt in West Iceland is a rewarding self-guided tour. This historic site was the home of Snorri Sturluson, one of Iceland's most important historical figures, and visitors can look around the area while learning about his life and works. A walking path takes visitors through the village, past Snorralaug, a geothermal pool that dates back to the 13th century. Information signs provide details about Snorri's life and the significance of Reykholt in Icelandic history.

CHAPTER 11

HIDDEN GEMS AND OFFBEAT ADVENTURES

Off the Beaten Paths

Iceland is renowned for its breathtaking landscapes, from towering waterfalls and volcanic craters to glaciers and fjords. While many of its most famous sights are often busy with tourists, the true essence of Iceland can often be found along the quieter, less-traveled paths. These off-the-beaten-track locations offer a sense of isolation, raw beauty, and serenity, allowing travelers to experience the untouched wonders of the country in a more intimate and personal way. Exploring these hidden gems and less-visited trails can provide visitors with a deeper connection to Iceland's unique landscapes and history, far from the crowds that gather around popular spots.

One such area that offers a sense of remote beauty is the Westfjords. This region, located in the northwest of Iceland, is a paradise for those seeking solitude and awe-inspiring landscapes. The fjords, with their steep cliffs, deep blue waters, and jagged coastlines, are a stark reminder of Iceland's raw natural beauty. The Westfjords are home to a number of less-frequented hiking trails that take visitors through some of the country's most dramatic scenery. A notable destination is Hornstrandir Nature Reserve, one of the most remote and pristine areas in Iceland. Accessible only by boat during the summer months, Hornstrandir offers a network of hiking trails that meander through untouched wilderness. This reserve is known for its abundant birdlife, including puffins and arctic foxes, which roam freely in the area. Walking here is an immersive experience in the quiet isolation of nature, where visitors can look around rugged cliffs, wildflower-covered meadows, and tranquil valleys, all without encountering many other travelers. The lack of infrastructure in Hornstrandir means that hikers must be well-prepared, carrying all necessary supplies, but the reward is an unparalleled sense of adventure and connection to the land.

In the southern highlands, Landmannalaugar is often included on the itineraries of those seeking more adventurous paths, but there are lesser-known trails in this geothermal region that offer equally stunning views without the crowds. While the Laugavegur Trail is famous, the Hrafntinnusker to Landmannalaugar route offers a more remote experience. This trail winds through striking rhyolite mountains, geothermal hot springs, and expansive lava fields. Along the way, travelers can enjoy the brilliant colors of the mountains, with shades of red, orange, yellow, and green created by volcanic activity over thousands of years. This area is a geologist's dream, with active hot springs and steam rising from the ground in various places. Taking time to look around beyond the main trails allows visitors to find out hidden spots where the earth's geothermal power is on full display. Walking through these volcanic landscapes provides a surreal experience, with few signs of human interference, allowing visitors to fully appreciate Iceland's untamed beauty.

The Eastfjords region of Iceland is another area that remains relatively unlook around by the majority of tourists. Characterized by quiet fishing villages, towering mountains, and deep fjords, the Eastfjords are ideal for those looking to venture off the main tourist path. One such walk in this region is the hike up to Hengifoss, one of Iceland's tallest waterfalls. Located near the town of Egilsstaðir, the trail to Hengifoss is a peaceful trip along a river, where visitors pass through green greenery and basalt cliffs. The waterfall itself is a spectacular sight, cascading down over 120 meters into a gorge, with layers of red clay sandwiched between black basalt rock. For those willing to continue beyond Hengifoss, further trails lead into remote valleys where few tourists venture, providing a more personal and secluded experience with Iceland's dramatic landscapes.

A particularly magical off-the-beaten-path destination is the Þórsmörk valley, located between the glaciers Eyjafjallajökull and Mýrdalsjökull. While Þórsmörk is accessible by tour buses, there are many areas in the valley where you can find peace and quiet, particularly on the lesser-used hiking trails. The valley is an oasis of greenery, with birch forests, glacial rivers, and stunning mountain views. Walking through Þórsmörk, hikers can look around trails that range from easy strolls through meadows to challenging hikes up to high mountain passes. One rewarding walk is the trek to the Valahnúkur viewpoint, which offers a panoramic view of the valley, glaciers, and nearby volcanoes. The isolation and tranquility of Þórsmörk are what make it a special destination for hikers seeking a more intimate experience with Iceland's diverse terrain.

Another hidden gem is Borgarfjörður Eystri, located in the northeast of Iceland. This area is known for its stunning hiking opportunities, with trails that take visitors through colorful rhyolite mountains, quiet valleys, and along dramatic coastlines. The Víknaslóðir trail, also known as the "Deserted Inlets Trek," is one of the most scenic hiking routes in this region. It offers a trip through some of the most remote parts of Iceland, where visitors can experience the country's untouched wilderness. Along the way, hikers pass by abandoned farms, remote beaches, and high mountain ridges, all with breathtaking views of the surrounding landscapes. Borgarfjörður Eystri is also famous for its rich folklore, particularly stories about elves and other mystical beings. Exploring this region on foot allows visitors to connect with both the natural beauty and the cultural history of Iceland's more secluded corners.

The Snæfellsnes Peninsula, often referred to as "Iceland in miniature" due to its diverse landscapes, is another area where visitors can find hidden walking trails. While sites like Kirkjufell and Snæfellsjökull are well-known, there are many lesser-visited paths that offer equally impressive views. One such walk is the Hellnar to Arnarstapi coastal path, a quiet route that follows the rugged coastline along the base of Snæfellsjökull. The trail winds through lava fields, past sea cliffs teeming with birdlife, and offers stunning views of the ocean and nearby mountains. This walk is particularly rewarding at sunrise or sunset when the light casts a golden glow over the landscape. For those seeking an even more remote experience, there are trails that lead to isolated beaches and lava fields further inland, where the stillness of the landscape allows visitors to feel completely disconnected from the outside world.

Iceland's Vatnajökull National Park, home to Europe's largest glacier, also offers plenty of opportunities for off-the-beaten-path exploration. While glacier hikes are popular, there are quieter trails that take visitors through glacial valleys, along remote rivers, and into hidden canyons. One such destination is Skaftafell, a nature reserve within the park that is home to lesser-known walks such as the hike to Kristínartindar. This trail offers an exceptional view of the glacier, as well as the surrounding mountains and valleys. The remote beauty of Skaftafell, combined with its accessibility, makes it a perfect location for those seeking solitude in nature.

Finally, for those looking to truly escape the beaten path, the central highlands of Iceland offer some of the country's most rugged and remote landscapes. Accessible only during the summer months, the highlands are a vast, uninhabited area of mountains, deserts, and volcanic landscapes. One of the best ways to look around the highlands is by hiking in the Kerlingarfjöll mountain range. These striking mountains, known for their colorful rhyolite peaks and geothermal activity, offer several walking trails that take visitors deep into this remote wilderness. The silence and vastness of the highlands create an almost otherworldly atmosphere, making it a perfect destination for those seeking true adventure far from civilization.

Iceland is a country that rewards those who are willing to step off the main tourist path and look around its quieter, less-visited areas. From the fjords of the Westfjords to the volcanic landscapes of the central highlands, these off-the-beaten-track walks and destinations offer a unique and intimate way to experience the country's natural beauty. Whether hiking through remote nature reserves, walking along quiet coastlines, or venturing into the untouched wilderness of the highlands, travelers who seek out these hidden gems will find that Iceland's true magic often lies in its less-traveled corners. By exploring these quieter paths, visitors can experience the raw, untamed beauty of Iceland in a way that feels personal and immersive, far from the busy crowds of the more popular attractions.

Hidden Gems

Iceland, with its vast landscapes of volcanic terrain, glaciers, waterfalls, and rugged coastlines, is a country that offers some of the most well-known natural wonders in the world. However, beyond the famous spots like the Blue Lagoon, the Golden Circle, and the waterfalls of the South Coast, there are countless hidden gems scattered across the island. These lesser-known places offer an incredible opportunity for tourists to experience the quieter, more untouched parts of Iceland, where the beauty is just as magnificent, but the crowds are far smaller. For those willing to look around a little further, these hidden gems offer the chance to connect with Iceland's landscapes and culture in a deeper, more personal way.

One of the true hidden gems in Iceland is Gjáin, a small valley in the Þjórsárdalur region of southern Iceland. Gjáin is a magical oasis, with green green vegetation, small waterfalls, and lava formations that make it feel like a world away from the harsher, more volcanic landscapes for which Iceland is famous. Although it is not as well-known as some of the bigger attractions, Gjáin is a perfect place for a peaceful walk, surrounded by natural beauty. The area is relatively easy to access by car, but the quiet and serenity of the valley often means visitors will have the place almost entirely to themselves. Nearby, tourists can also visit the ruins of Stöng, a reconstructed Viking-age longhouse that was buried by volcanic ash in 1104. Together, Gjáin and Stöng offer a glimpse into both Iceland's natural beauty and its Viking history, making them a must-see for anyone interested in the quieter, more historical side of the country.

Further east, another hidden gem lies in the remote highlands: Kerlingarfjöll. This mountain range, located in the heart of Iceland, is an otherworldly landscape of geothermal activity, steep peaks, and colorful rhyolite mountains. The region is much less visited than other highland areas like Landmannalaugar, which makes it a fantastic destination for those seeking adventure and solitude. The geothermal area in Kerlingarfjöll is particularly striking, with steam rising from the ground, hot springs, and boiling mud pots dotting the landscape. Visitors can hike through the region, crossing rivers and climbing ridges that offer breathtaking views of the surrounding mountains and glaciers. The remote location and rugged terrain of Kerlingarfjöll give it an almost mystical feel, making it one of Iceland's true hidden treasures.

On the west coast of Iceland, the Snæfellsnes Peninsula is often referred to as "Iceland in Miniature" because it contains such a diverse range of landscapes, including glaciers, lava fields, cliffs, and beaches. While some parts of the peninsula, such as Kirkjufell Mountain, are well-known, there are many hidden gems here that are often overlooked by tourists. One such place is Ytri Tunga Beach, a small, unassuming beach where visitors can watch seals basking on the rocks. The beach is off the beaten path, and while it may not have the dramatic landscapes of some of Iceland's other coastal areas, the chance to observe seals in their natural habitat is a special experience. Nearby, the small fishing villages of Arnarstapi and Hellnar offer quiet places to walk along the coast, with stunning views of the sea and the towering Snæfellsjökull glacier in the background.

Another lesser-known gem is Hraunfossar, a series of waterfalls located in west Iceland. Hraunfossar is unique in that the water flows out from underneath a lava field, cascading gently over a series of ledges into the Hvítá river. The result is a beautiful and serene scene, with clear, blue water flowing over black lava rocks and surrounded by green vegetation. A short walk from Hraunfossar brings visitors to Barnafoss, a much more turbulent waterfall that rushes through a narrow gorge. These waterfalls are not as large or famous as Gullfoss or Skógafoss, but their beauty and the peaceful atmosphere make them well worth a visit for those who enjoy quieter, less crowded destinations.

In the far east of Iceland, the Stórurð area is one of the country's most remote and least-visited hiking destinations. Located in the shadow of the Dyrfjöll mountains, Stórurð is a hidden valley filled with giant boulders, glacial pools, and green moss-covered hills. The hike to Stórurð is challenging but incredibly rewarding, with stunning views of the surrounding mountains and the chance to look around a landscape that feels like something out of a fantasy novel. The crystal-clear pools of water in Stórurð are particularly beautiful, and during the summer months, the area is blanketed with wildflowers. Because of its remote location, Stórurð sees very few visitors, making it an ideal destination for those seeking solitude and natural beauty away from the usual tourist spots.

On the south coast of Iceland, most tourists flock to popular spots like Seljalandsfoss and Reynisfjara Beach, but just off the main road lies the small village of Vík í Mýrdal, which offers a few hidden gems of its own. One of these is the Reynisdrangar sea stacks, towering rock formations that rise out of the ocean just off the coast of Vík. While many people stop to view the sea stacks from a distance, few take the time to walk along the black sand beach and get up close to these dramatic rock formations. The beach here is quieter and less crowded than the more famous Reynisfjara, but the scenery is just as stunning. Nearby, the Dyrhólaey peninsula offers a fantastic viewpoint over the surrounding coastline, with sweeping views of the sea, cliffs, and the Mýrdalsjökull glacier in the distance.

In the north of Iceland, the Krafla volcanic area is another hidden gem that offers visitors the chance to look around one of the country's most active volcanic regions. The Krafla caldera is home to a series of volcanic craters, geothermal fields, and lava flows, all of which can be look aroundd on foot via a network of hiking trails. One of the highlights of the area is the Viti Crater, a turquoise-colored geothermal lake that sits inside a large volcanic crater. The area around Krafla is much less visited than the geothermal areas in the south of Iceland, making it a perfect destination for those interested in exploring Iceland's volcanic landscape without the crowds.

Another hidden gem for those interested in history and culture is the Eldheimar Museum on the island of Heimaey, part of the Vestmannaeyjar (Westman Islands) archipelago. This museum tells the story of the 1973 volcanic eruption that buried much of the island under lava and ash. The museum is built around one of the houses that was excavated from the ash, providing visitors with a unique look at the aftermath of the eruption. Heimaey itself is a hidden gem, with beautiful cliffs, birdlife (including puffins), and a fascinating history of volcanic activity. The island is accessible by ferry, and visitors can hike to the top of Eldfell, the volcano that erupted in 1973, for stunning views of the surrounding islands and the mainland.
Finally, for those willing to venture into the far north, the Ásbyrgi Canyon in the Vatnajökull National Park is one of Iceland's most spectacular and least-visited natural wonders.

This horseshoe-shaped canyon is surrounded by towering cliffs and filled with green vegetation, including birch trees and wildflowers. According to Icelandic folklore, Ásbyrgi was formed by the hoofprint of Odin's eight-legged horse, Sleipnir, and the canyon has a mystical, almost otherworldly atmosphere. There are several walking trails that allow visitors to look around the canyon, including a path that leads to a serene pond at the base of the cliffs. The quiet beauty of Ásbyrgi, combined with its remote location, makes it one of Iceland's most magical hidden gems.

Scenic Lookout Points

Iceland is known for its incredible natural beauty, and one of the best ways to appreciate it is by visiting the many scenic lookout points scattered across the country. These vantage points offer breathtaking views of Iceland's diverse landscapes, from towering glaciers and volcanoes to dramatic cliffs and endless coastlines. Whether you are driving along the country's famous Ring Road or venturing into its more remote regions, there are countless spots where you can pause and take in the stunning surroundings. Each lookout point provides a different perspective on Iceland's unique geology, wildlife, and weather, making these stops essential for any traveler who wants to fully experience the country's natural wonders.

One of the most iconic scenic lookout points in Iceland is the view from Dyrhólaey, a promontory on the south coast. From this vantage point, visitors are treated to sweeping views of the black sand beaches stretching along the coast, the dramatic basalt sea stacks of Reynisdrangar rising out of the ocean, and the vast expanse of the Atlantic Ocean. Dyrhólaey is also a prime spot for birdwatching, particularly during the summer months when puffins nest in the cliffs. Standing at the edge of the cliffs, looking out over the rugged coastline and the crashing waves below, gives you a sense of the immense power and beauty of Iceland's natural landscape. The contrast between the black sand, the blue sea, and the green green cliffs makes this viewpoint one of the most photogenic in the country.

Further east, along the same stretch of coastline, is another must-visit lookout point: the Fjaðrárgljúfur Canyon. This 100-meter-deep, 2-kilometer-long canyon was carved out by glacial meltwater thousands of years ago and is now one of Iceland's hidden gems. The canyon walls are steep and covered in moss, with the Fjaðrá River winding through the valley below. Visitors can walk along the rim of the canyon, stopping at various viewpoints to gaze down at the river and the green greenery that lines the canyon floor. The views from Fjaðrárgljúfur are especially striking in the early morning or late afternoon when the sunlight casts a golden glow over the landscape. This lookout point offers a sense of peaceful isolation, far from the busier tourist destinations, allowing visitors to fully appreciate the raw, untouched beauty of Iceland's interior.

In the western part of Iceland, the Snæfellsnes Peninsula offers some of the most dramatic scenic viewpoints in the country. One such viewpoint is the Saxhóll Crater, which sits within the Snæfellsjökull National Park. The crater, which is the remnant of a now-dormant volcano, provides panoramic views of the surrounding landscape, including the Snæfellsjökull glacier and the rugged coastline of the peninsula. Visitors can hike up a set of stairs to the top of the crater, where they are rewarded with a 360-degree view of the volcanic landscape that stretches out in every direction. On a clear day, the view extends all the way to the Atlantic Ocean, making this a perfect spot for photography and nature lovers alike. The sense of being surrounded by ancient volcanic formations and glaciers gives visitors a deeper appreciation of the geological forces that have shaped Iceland over millennia.

Another unforgettable scenic lookout point is the view from Valahnúkur in Þórsmörk, a remote valley surrounded by glaciers and mountains. The hike to the top of Valahnúkur is short but steep, and the effort is well worth it for the stunning views at the summit. From the top, visitors can see the entire Þórsmörk valley, with its green birch forests, glacial rivers, and snow-capped mountains in the distance. The contrast between the green greenery of the valley and the stark, icy peaks of the surrounding glaciers creates a truly breathtaking scene. Þórsmörk is one of Iceland's most remote and beautiful areas, and the view from Valahnúkur is the perfect way to experience its vastness and isolation.

In the north of Iceland, Goðafoss is a waterfall that offers one of the most beautiful lookout points in the country. Known as the "Waterfall of the Gods," Goðafoss is a semicircular waterfall where the Skjálfandafljót River cascades over a series of cliffs into a wide, shallow pool below. Visitors can view the waterfall from several different vantage points, including both sides of the river and a small island in the middle of the falls. Each viewpoint offers a different perspective on the waterfall, and the sound of the rushing water, combined with the mist rising from the pool below, creates a powerful sensory experience. The views from Goðafoss are especially stunning in the winter when the waterfall is partially frozen, creating an otherworldly landscape of ice and water.

For those traveling along the Golden Circle, the viewpoint at Kerið Crater offers a unique glimpse into Iceland's volcanic past. Kerið is a volcanic crater lake that was formed around 3,000 years ago, and its deep blue water is surrounded by steep red volcanic rock. Visitors can walk along the rim of the crater or descend into the bowl to get closer to the lake itself. The contrast between the blue water, the red rocks, and the green moss that grows along the crater walls creates a stunning visual effect, and the view from the top of the crater is one of the most striking in the region.

Another must-see lookout point in the Golden Circle area is the view from Geysir. The geothermal area around Geysir is famous for its hot springs and geysers, including Strokkur, which erupts every few minutes, sending a column of water and steam high into the air. Visitors can watch the eruptions from a safe distance, but the best views are from the small hills surrounding the geothermal field, where you can see the steam rising from the various hot springs and geysers scattered across the landscape. The combination of the geothermal activity, the surrounding mountains, and the blue sky creates a scene that is both otherworldly and quintessentially Icelandic.

In the Eastfjords region, the Hengifoss waterfall provides another spectacular scenic viewpoint. Hengifoss is one of the tallest waterfalls in Iceland, with water cascading over 120 meters into a deep canyon below. The waterfall is framed by layers of red clay and black basalt rock, creating a striking visual contrast. The hike to Hengifoss takes visitors along a well-marked trail that follows the river up to the base of the falls. Along the way, there are several lookout points where visitors can stop and take in the view of the waterfall and the surrounding canyon. The scenery here is both dramatic and peaceful, making Hengifoss a perfect spot for those looking to escape the more crowded tourist destinations.

For visitors to the Vatnajökull National Park, the view from Skaftafell offers some of the most stunning glacier views in Iceland. Skaftafell is located at the foot of the Vatnajökull glacier, Europe's largest ice cap, and the lookout point offers a panoramic view of the glacier, the surrounding mountains, and the vast expanses of ice and snow that stretch as far as the eye can see. The park is also home to several other notable lookout points, including the view of Svartifoss, a waterfall surrounded by dark basalt columns that give the falls a unique and striking appearance. The combination of glaciers, waterfalls, and volcanic landscapes makes Skaftafell one of the most visually impressive areas in Iceland, and the views from its lookout points are truly unforgettable.

Local Myths, Legends, and Folklore

Iceland is a country steeped in myth, legend, and folklore, with stories that have been passed down through generations. These tales are deeply woven into the cultural fabric of Iceland, reflecting the island's dramatic landscapes, harsh environment, and the deep connection its people have with the natural world. For visitors, learning about Iceland's rich folklore offers a window into the country's history and mindset, as well as an opportunity to look around the magical and mystical elements that continue to influence the way Icelanders view their surroundings. From tales of elves and trolls to sagas of Viking heroes and supernatural forces, Icelandic folklore provides a captivating glimpse into the country's soul.

One of the most famous aspects of Icelandic folklore is the belief in huldufólk, or "hidden people." These beings are said to live in rocks, hills, and caves, hidden from human view, but their presence is felt in many parts of Iceland. Huldufólk are often described as similar to humans in appearance, but they possess magical powers and can influence the world around them. According to tradition, they prefer to remain unseen, but they sometimes interact with humans, either helping or hindering them depending on how they are treated. In Iceland, it is not uncommon for people to go out of their way to avoid disturbing areas where huldufólk are believed to live. For example, road construction projects have been altered or delayed to avoid moving or damaging rocks that are thought to be homes for hidden people. While belief in huldufólk is not as widespread as it once was, it still holds a special place in the hearts of many Icelanders, and visitors will find that stories of the hidden people are still told with respect and wonder.

Another key figure in Icelandic folklore is the troll, a giant and often fearsome creature that lives in the mountains and rocky landscapes of Iceland. Trolls are usually depicted as large, slow-witted beings who can be dangerous to humans if crossed. However, they are also vulnerable to sunlight, and many of Iceland's rock formations are said to be the petrified remains of trolls who were caught outside when the sun rose, turning them to stone. One famous example of this is the Reynisdrangar sea stacks near the village of Vík. According to legend, these towering basalt columns are the remnants of two trolls who were pulling a three-masted ship towards land. They were caught by the rising sun and turned to stone, where they remain to this day, standing just off the shore. Visitors to Iceland will encounter many rock formations and natural features that are tied to stories of trolls, giving the landscape an almost magical quality, as though the mountains and cliffs themselves are alive with ancient secrets.

Icelandic folklore is also filled with stories of ghosts and supernatural beings. The island's long, dark winters and remote landscapes have fostered a tradition of ghost stories that often reflect the isolation and hardship of life in Iceland. Many of these tales involve spirits who return from the dead to haunt the living, seeking revenge or justice for wrongs done to them in life. One well-known story is that of Djákninn á Myrká, or "The Deacon of Dark River." In this tale, a deacon is riding to meet his lover one winter night when he falls into a river and drowns. His body is found and buried, but his spirit rises and rides to meet his lover as planned. When she realizes that he is dead, she escapes his grasp just as he tries to drag her into the grave with him. This chilling story, like many Icelandic ghost tales, is a reflection of the harsh realities of life in a land where death was always close at hand, whether from the freezing cold, the unpredictable sea, or the volatile landscape.

The Icelandic sagas, though not strictly folklore, are another important part of the country's storytelling tradition. These epic tales, written down in the 13th century but based on oral traditions that date back to the Viking Age, tell the stories of Iceland's early settlers, their struggles, and their adventures. The sagas are filled with larger-than-life characters, heroic deeds, and battles, but they also include elements of the supernatural. In the sagas, heroes often encounter strange and magical beings, and their fates are sometimes influenced by forces beyond their control. One of the most famous sagas is the Saga of Egil Skallagrímsson, which tells the story of a Viking warrior and poet who battles both enemies and his own inner demons. The sagas are revered in Iceland and are still studied and enjoyed today, offering a deep connection to the country's Viking past and the enduring power of storytelling.

Another key figure in Icelandic folklore is the Jólakötturinn, or "Yule Cat." This fearsome creature is said to roam the countryside during the Christmas season, devouring anyone who has not received new clothes to wear before Christmas Eve. The Yule Cat is tied to the tradition of giving and receiving new clothes for Christmas, a practice that was once seen as a way of ensuring that everyone, even the poorest members of society, had something warm to wear during the cold winter months. The legend of the Yule Cat is still told in Iceland today, often as a way of encouraging children to behave well and help with chores in the lead-up to Christmas. Alongside the Yule Cat are the Yule Lads, a group of mischievous figures who visit children during the 13 days leading up to Christmas. Each Yule Lad has his own distinct personality and habits, ranging from stealing food to slamming doors, but they also leave small gifts in the shoes of well-behaved children.

Iceland's unique geography has also inspired many tales of sea monsters and mysterious creatures that inhabit its waters. One famous example is the Lagarfljótsormur, a serpent-like creature said to live in Lagarfljót, a lake in east Iceland. The Lagarfljótsormur is often compared to Scotland's Loch Ness Monster, with sightings of a long, snake-like creature in the water reported for centuries. The earliest recorded mention of the Lagarfljótsormur dates back to the 14th century, and while scientific explanations have been offered for the sightings, the legend remains a popular topic of discussion among locals and visitors alike.

In addition to mythical creatures, Icelandic folklore is also rich with stories of magic and sorcery. Iceland was once home to a strong tradition of magic, particularly during the medieval period, when practitioners of seiðr, a type of Norse magic, were believed to have the power to shape the world around them. Many of Iceland's medieval manuscripts include spells, charms, and runes designed to protect against evil, bring good fortune, or control the elements. The Museum of Icelandic Sorcery and Witchcraft, located in the town of Hólmavík, is dedicated to preserving this part of Iceland's history and showcases many of the magical symbols and rituals that were once used in Iceland. Visitors to the museum can learn about the dark history of sorcery in Iceland, including the infamous witch trials of the 17th century, when several men were accused of practicing magic and executed.

Finally, no tour of Icelandic folklore would be complete without mentioning the Álfhólar, or "elf hills," which are believed to be the homes of elves and other magical beings. These small, rocky hills are scattered throughout the Icelandic countryside, and it is said that disturbing them can bring bad luck. In some cases, roads or construction projects have been diverted to avoid damaging Álfhólar, and many Icelanders still treat these places with great respect. The belief in elves and other hidden beings is deeply ingrained in Icelandic culture, and even those who do not believe in the literal existence of these creatures often see the stories as a way of expressing a deep connection to the land and its mysteries.

Religious Sites and Pilgrimages

Iceland is a country where nature, culture, and spirituality have long been intertwined. Though Iceland is often more recognized for its natural wonders, such as its volcanoes, glaciers, and waterfalls, it also has a deep history of religious beliefs that have evolved over centuries. This history is reflected in the religious sites and traditions that dot the landscape, providing both spiritual insight and historical significance.

Christianity was introduced to Iceland around the year 1000, following the decision of the Althing (Iceland's national parliament) to adopt the new religion. However, Icelandic religious history goes back even further, to the time when Norse paganism was the dominant belief system. This duality of pagan and Christian traditions can still be felt today, as remnants of both religions continue to influence Icelandic society. For example, while most Icelanders today are Christian, many also maintain a strong cultural connection to the old Norse gods and traditions.

One of the most important religious sites in Iceland is **Skálholt**, a small town that played a pivotal role in the history of Icelandic Christianity. Located in the south of Iceland, Skálholt was the center of Iceland's religious, cultural, and political life from the 11th century until the Reformation in the 16th century. It was here that Iceland's first bishop, Ísleifur Gissurarson, established a school and cathedral, making Skálholt the most important religious center in the country for centuries. The original cathedral was destroyed in an earthquake in 1784, but the site has been reconstructed, and today, visitors can look around the modern **Skálholt Cathedral**, which was built in the 20th century. The cathedral's interior is simple yet striking, with beautiful stained-glass windows and a peaceful atmosphere that reflects the spiritual history of the site. Visitors can also look around the archaeological remains of the earlier cathedral, as well as the grave of Jón Arason, the last Catholic bishop of Iceland, who was executed during the Reformation. For those interested in Iceland's Christian heritage, Skálholt is a must-visit destination, offering a glimpse into the country's religious evolution and the central role that the church played in its early development.

Another important Christian site is the **Reykholt Church** in the **Borgarfjörður** region. Reykholt was once the home of **Snorri Sturluson**, one of Iceland's most famous historical figures, who was a poet, historian, and politician in the 13th century. Although Snorri was not a religious figure, his writings, including the **Prose Edda**, played a crucial role in preserving Icelandic mythology and history. The modern Reykholt Church, built near Snorri's home, is an important cultural and religious site that honors Iceland's literary and religious past. Visitors can also see **Snorralaug**, a hot spring that Snorri is believed to have used for bathing, as well as the remnants of his medieval farmstead. The church itself is a beautiful and peaceful place, surrounded by the rolling hills of the Borgarfjörður countryside, making it a serene destination for those seeking reflection or a deeper connection to Iceland's past.

While Christianity is the dominant religion in Iceland today, the country's pagan past is still an integral part of its cultural identity. In recent years, there has been a resurgence of interest in **Ásatrú**, the modern revival of the Old Norse religion. This movement, which is recognized as an official religion in Iceland, celebrates the ancient gods and goddesses of Norse mythology, such as **Óðinn**, **Þór**, and **Freyja**. Ásatrú ceremonies, known as **blót**, are held at various sacred sites across the country, often in connection with the natural landscape, such as waterfalls, mountains, and forests. These ceremonies focus on themes of nature, community, and respect for the land, reflecting the deep connection that Icelanders have with their environment. One important site for modern Ásatrú practitioners is **Þingvellir**, the historic site of Iceland's first parliament and a place of great spiritual significance. Þingvellir is also home to **Lögberg**, the Law Rock, where the laws of the land were recited in ancient times. For visitors interested in learning more about Iceland's pagan roots, Þingvellir offers a powerful connection to both the country's legal and religious history.

In addition to these Christian and pagan sites, there are also important pilgrimage routes in Iceland that have been used by both locals and visitors for centuries. One of the most famous is the **Pilgrimage of Jón Arason**, which traces the trip of the last Catholic bishop of Iceland, who was executed during the Reformation. This pilgrimage route begins at Hólar, the ancient episcopal seat in northern Iceland, and follows the path that Jón Arason took when he was captured and taken to Skálholt, where he was later beheaded. The pilgrimage is a reminder of the turbulent period of the Reformation in Iceland, when Catholicism was replaced by Lutheranism, and it offers pilgrims a chance to reflect on the country's religious history while traversing some of its most beautiful landscapes.

Another important pilgrimage destination is **Hólar í Hjaltadal**, located in the north of Iceland. Hólar was the episcopal seat for the northern part of the country for over 700 years and was a center of religious learning and culture.

The cathedral at Hólar, built in the 18th century, is one of the oldest stone buildings in Iceland and remains an important religious site today. Pilgrims and tourists alike can visit the cathedral, as well as the nearby **Hólar University College**, which continues the site's long tradition of education and learning. The peaceful surroundings of Hólar, with its quiet valleys and mountains, make it an ideal place for reflection and spiritual renewal.

Another interesting religious site in Iceland is the **Víkingaheimar Museum**, located near **Keflavík**. While not a traditional religious site, the museum showcases the **Íslendingur**, a replica of a Viking ship that was used to recreate the trip of Leif Erikson to North America. For those interested in Iceland's Viking history and the spiritual beliefs of the Norse look arounders who first settled the island, Víkingaheimar provides a fascinating look at the intersection of religion, exploration, and mythology. The museum also highlights the role that Christianity played in the later Viking Age, as many of the settlers who arrived in Iceland were pagan, but gradually converted to Christianity.

While Iceland may not have as many religious pilgrimage routes as other countries, it is a land deeply rooted in spirituality, with religious sites that reflect both its Christian heritage and its pagan past. Whether visiting ancient churches, exploring the modern revival of Norse paganism, or walking in the footsteps of historical figures like Jón Arason, travelers to Iceland can gain a deeper understanding of the country's complex and multifaceted religious history. Each of these sites offers not only a glimpse into the past but also a chance to reflect on the spiritual connections that have shaped Iceland's identity.

Road Trip Routes and Scenic Drives

Iceland is a land of stunning landscapes, where every turn in the road can reveal a new and breathtaking view. For tourists seeking to experience the beauty of this island nation, road trips offer one of the best ways to look around at your own pace, allowing for flexibility and a deeper connection to the landscape. Iceland's road trip routes and scenic drives are famous for taking travelers through diverse natural wonders, from towering glaciers and volcanoes to rugged coastlines, geothermal hot spots, and cascading waterfalls.

The most iconic road trip in Iceland is the **Ring Road**, or **Route 1**, which circles the entire country. Spanning around 1,332 kilometers (828 miles), the Ring Road is the ultimate route for those looking to experience a little bit of everything Iceland has to offer. It passes through some of the country's most famous attractions, including the powerful **Dettifoss** waterfall, the **Jökulsárlón** glacier lagoon, and the **Skaftafell** National Park. The route takes you through both urban areas, such as **Reykjavík** and **Akureyri**, as well as remote stretches of unspoiled nature where you may not see another vehicle for miles. Travelers can take their time along the Ring Road, stopping at small villages, black sand beaches, lava fields, and more. It's recommended to spend at least a week on this trip to fully appreciate everything the route has to offer, although some tourists prefer to stretch it out even longer. The Ring Road is mostly paved and accessible year-round, though it's important to note that winter driving conditions can be difficult, especially in the north and east of the country.

For those looking for a shorter but equally scenic drive, the **Golden Circle** route is a popular choice. This route takes visitors through some of the most famous natural landmarks in Iceland and is easily accessible from Reykjavík, making it perfect for a day trip. The Golden Circle includes three main stops: **Þingvellir National Park**, **Geysir**, and **Gullfoss** waterfall. Þingvellir is not only a site of historical significance, being the location of Iceland's first parliament, but it's also a geological marvel, where the Eurasian and North American tectonic plates meet. Geysir is home to the famous **Strokkur** geyser, which erupts every few minutes, sending a plume of boiling water high into the air. Finally, Gullfoss, one of Iceland's most famous waterfalls, offers visitors the chance to witness the raw power of nature as water from the **Hvítá River** plunges into a deep canyon. The Golden Circle route is approximately 300 kilometers (190 miles) in total and can be completed in a single day, although many travelers choose to spend more time exploring the sights along the way.

For those who want to experience the less-traveled parts of Iceland, the **Westfjords** offer an incredible road trip experience that is truly off the beaten path. The roads in the Westfjords are winding and narrow, and the region's remoteness means that it receives far fewer visitors than other parts of Iceland. However, those who make the trip are rewarded with some of the most dramatic scenery in the country. The **Dynjandi** waterfall, often considered one of the most beautiful in Iceland, is a must-see stop along the route.

The waterfall cascades down a series of tiers, creating a stunning fan-shaped flow of water. The Westfjords are also home to the **Látrabjarg** cliffs, which are the westernmost point of Europe and a prime spot for birdwatching, particularly for puffins. The drive through the Westfjords can be challenging, especially in winter, so it's recommended for experienced drivers who are comfortable with Iceland's rugged terrain. This region is best visited in the summer months when the weather is more favorable, and the roads are more accessible.

Another popular road trip route is the **Snæfellsnes Peninsula**, often referred to as "Iceland in Miniature" because it offers a little bit of everything that makes Iceland unique. This 90-kilometer-long peninsula is home to **Snæfellsjökull**, a glacier-topped volcano that served as the inspiration for Jules Verne's novel *Trip to the Center of the Earth*. The Snæfellsnes Peninsula is dotted with charming fishing villages, dramatic cliffs, and black sand beaches. One of the most iconic sights along the route is **Kirkjufell**, a mountain that has become famous for its distinctive shape and has been featured in many photographs and films. Near the town of **Arnarstapi**, visitors can look around a stunning coastline of basalt cliffs and sea arches, where the Atlantic waves crash dramatically against the shore. The Snæfellsnes Peninsula is easily accessible from Reykjavík and can be look aroundd in a day or two, making it an ideal option for travelers who want a scenic road trip without committing to a longer trip.

For those who want to look around Iceland's east coast, the **Eastfjords** provide a beautiful and less-traveled route that offers breathtaking views of fjords, mountains, and tiny fishing villages. The roads here wind through narrow valleys and along steep cliffs, offering travelers some of the most scenic drives in Iceland. One highlight of the Eastfjords is the town of **Seyðisfjörður**, a picturesque village nestled at the end of a fjord and surrounded by snow-capped mountains. The town is known for its colorful wooden houses, vibrant art scene, and its connection to the ferry service that links Iceland to mainland Europe. Another must-see spot along this route is **Hengifoss**, one of the tallest waterfalls in Iceland, with red clay and black basalt columns creating a striking contrast behind the cascade of water. The Eastfjords offer a peaceful and quiet alternative to the more popular tourist routes, and travelers who make the trip are rewarded with some of the most dramatic and untouched scenery in Iceland.

In the north of Iceland, the **Diamond Circle** is another spectacular driving route that takes visitors through some of the country's most iconic natural attractions. The Diamond Circle includes stops at **Lake Mývatn**, **Dettifoss** waterfall, **Ásbyrgi Canyon**, and the town of **Húsavík**, known as the whale-watching capital of Iceland. Lake Mývatn is famous for its unique geological formations, including the **Dimmuborgir** lava fields and the **Krafla** volcanic crater. Dettifoss, one of the most powerful waterfalls in Europe, is a truly awe-inspiring sight as it plunges into the canyon below with incredible force. Ásbyrgi Canyon, with its horseshoe-shaped walls, is a tranquil and beautiful spot that is steeped in Norse mythology, as it is said to have been formed by the hoofprint of **Sleipnir**, the eight-legged horse of the god Odin.

The Diamond Circle route is around 260 kilometers (160 miles) and can be completed in a day, though many travelers choose to spend more time in the area to fully look around the sights.

For those looking to look around the southern coast of Iceland, the drive along **Route 1** from Reykjavík to the town of **Vík** is one of the most popular scenic drives in the country. This route takes travelers past some of Iceland's most famous landmarks, including **Seljalandsfoss** and **Skógafoss** waterfalls, the **Reynisfjara** black sand beach, and the **Sólheimajökull** glacier. Seljalandsfoss is unique in that visitors can walk behind the waterfall, offering a completely different perspective and a chance to feel the mist from the falls up close. Skógafoss, one of the largest waterfalls in Iceland, is another must-see along the route, with a steep staircase leading to a viewpoint at the top of the falls. Reynisfjara, with its black sand and towering basalt columns, is one of the most iconic beaches in Iceland, though visitors should be cautious of the powerful waves that can make swimming dangerous. This stretch of road is easily accessible and is one of the best ways to experience Iceland's diverse landscapes in a short amount of time.

CHAPTER 12

SHOPPING AND SOUVENIRS

Shopping Districts and Malls

Iceland may be best known for its striking natural landscapes, but for tourists, exploring its shopping districts and malls offers an entirely different way to experience the country's unique culture and products. Whether you're looking for local crafts, traditional Icelandic clothing, high-end fashion, or souvenirs to take back home, Iceland has plenty of options for shoppers to look around. Though the country isn't as large or urbanized as some of its European neighbors, its capital Reykjavík and other towns provide a variety of shopping experiences that range from small, locally owned shops to modern malls.

Reykjavík, the capital and largest city of Iceland, is the main hub for shopping in the country. For tourists, Reykjavík's shopping districts are a great way to experience Icelandic design, fashion, and craftsmanship. One of the most popular and well-known shopping streets in the city is **Laugavegur**, which is the main shopping street in Reykjavík. Here, visitors will find a mix of high-end fashion boutiques, local designer shops, cozy cafés, and stores selling handmade goods and souvenirs. Laugavegur has a lively atmosphere, especially during the summer when the days are long, and visitors can spend hours wandering in and out of shops. Many of the stores on Laugavegur focus on Icelandic design and craftsmanship, offering products such as woolen goods, handmade jewelry, and locally sourced beauty products. **66°North**, an iconic Icelandic outerwear brand, has its flagship store on Laugavegur, and it's a must-visit for those looking for high-quality, stylish clothing that's built to withstand Iceland's unpredictable weather. Whether you're looking for a traditional Icelandic wool sweater (known as a **lopapeysa**), hand-knit scarves, or other locally made goods, Laugavegur is the place to start.

Close to Laugavegur, visitors can look around **Skólavörðustígur**, another popular shopping street in Reykjavík. This street is particularly known for its artsy and bohemian vibe, with a variety of small galleries, local craft shops, and boutiques selling Icelandic art, ceramics, and other handmade goods. Skólavörðustígur is also home to some of Reykjavík's best-known souvenir shops, where visitors can find traditional Icelandic products such as **volcanic rock jewelry**, **lava salt**, and **puffin figurines**. The street leads up to the iconic **Hallgrímskirkja Church**, so visitors can enjoy a scenic walk while shopping and take in one of the city's most recognizable landmarks. Skólavörðustígur has a more relaxed and intimate feel compared to the busier Laugavegur, making it a great spot for those who prefer a slower-paced shopping experience while supporting local artisans.

For tourists who are interested in luxury shopping and high-end fashion, **Kringlan Mall** in Reykjavík offers a more modern shopping experience. Kringlan is Iceland's largest shopping mall and features a wide range of international and local brands. Opened in 1987, the mall has expanded over the years and now boasts over 170 shops, restaurants, and services. Visitors to Kringlan can find well-known global brands such as **Zara**, **H&M**, **Nike**, and **Levi's**, as well as Icelandic fashion labels like **Farmers Market** and **Cintamani**. In addition to clothing, the mall has stores selling electronics, home goods, beauty products, and more. Kringlan is also home to a cinema, several restaurants, and a food court, making it a popular destination for both locals and tourists looking for a full day of shopping and entertainment. The mall is easily accessible from downtown Reykjavík, either by car or public transportation, and it provides a convenient indoor shopping experience, especially during the colder months when outdoor shopping may be less appealing.

Another popular shopping center in Reykjavík is **Smáralind**, located in the suburb of Kópavogur, just a short drive from the city center. Smáralind is the second-largest shopping mall in Iceland and offers a similar mix of international and local brands as Kringlan. With over 90 stores, the mall includes fashion retailers, electronics shops, beauty salons, and a large supermarket. One of the highlights of Smáralind is its focus on family-friendly amenities, with a large play area for children, as well as plenty of dining options ranging from casual cafés to full-service restaurants. Smáralind also has a cinema, making it a great destination for families or those looking for entertainment after a day of shopping. Like Kringlan, Smáralind provides a modern and comfortable shopping experience for those who prefer indoor malls, especially during Iceland's cold winters.

While Reykjavík is undoubtedly the center of shopping in Iceland, other parts of the country also offer unique shopping experiences, particularly for those looking for local crafts and handmade goods. In the town of **Akureyri**, often called the "Capital of the North," visitors can find a charming selection of local shops and boutiques. Akureyri's small-town atmosphere provides a more relaxed and intimate shopping experience compared to Reykjavík. The town is home to several shops selling Icelandic wool products, handcrafted jewelry, and other locally made goods. One of the highlights of shopping in Akureyri is the opportunity to find unique items that may not be available in larger stores in Reykjavík. Many of the shops in Akureyri are family-owned, and visitors can often meet the artisans and craftspeople behind the products. Akureyri's downtown area is compact and easy to look around on foot, making it a great destination for a day of leisurely shopping while taking in the town's picturesque setting on the shores of **Eyjafjörður** fjord.

For those visiting Iceland's east coast, the town of **Egilsstaðir** offers a small but charming shopping district with a focus on local crafts and products. Egilsstaðir is known for its proximity to Iceland's largest forest, **Hallormsstaðaskógur**, and its shops often reflect the region's connection to nature. Visitors can find a variety of handmade goods, including wooden carvings, ceramics, and other locally sourced products. The town also has a small but growing number of boutiques selling Icelandic fashion and woolen goods. Egilsstaðir is a great place to pick up unique souvenirs and gifts that reflect the natural beauty and craftsmanship of the region.

In addition to the shopping districts and malls, visitors to Iceland will also find plenty of opportunities to shop for local goods at **markets and festivals**. The **Kolaportið Flea Market** in Reykjavík is a must-visit for those looking for a more eclectic and budget-friendly shopping experience. Held on weekends in a large warehouse near the harbor, Kolaportið offers everything from second-hand clothing and vintage items to Icelandic delicacies like **dried fish** and **fermented shark**. It's also a great place to pick up unique souvenirs, including books, records, jewelry, and antiques. The market has a lively and busy atmosphere, with a mix of locals and tourists browsing the stalls. For those who enjoy treasure hunting and find outing hidden gems, Kolaportið is the perfect place to spend a few hours exploring.

For visitors interested in supporting local artisans and craftspeople, Iceland has a growing number of **artisan markets** and **craft fairs** that take place throughout the year. These markets often feature handmade goods, including jewelry, ceramics, textiles, and art, all created by local artists and designers. One of the most popular artisan markets in Reykjavík is the **Handverk og Hönnun** market, which showcases a wide variety of Icelandic design and craftsmanship. The market is usually held in conjunction with cultural festivals or during the holiday season, making it a great place to find unique gifts and souvenirs that are truly one-of-a-kind.

Iceland offers a diverse range of shopping experiences for tourists, from the busy streets of Reykjavík to the quiet towns and villages scattered across the country. The country's shopping districts and malls provide a window into Icelandic culture and design, with a focus on quality craftsmanship and sustainability.

When traveling to Iceland, exploring local markets can be one of the most enriching and memorable parts of the experience. While the country is best known for its incredible landscapes, geothermal wonders, and unique cultural heritage, its markets also offer a glimpse into Icelandic life and traditions. For tourists, these markets provide the opportunity to purchase handmade goods, local delicacies, and unique souvenirs that can't be found in larger commercial stores or malls.

One of the most famous markets in Iceland, particularly in Reykjavík, is the **Kolaportið Flea Market**, which is held every weekend near the old harbor. This indoor market has an eclectic mix of vendors selling everything from second-hand clothing and books to local Icelandic food products like dried fish, fermented shark, and traditional Icelandic sweets. It's one of the few places in the capital where you can truly find a mix of both the old and the new, with stalls offering vintage items alongside more modern crafts and souvenirs. For tourists, Kolaportið provides a relaxed, casual atmosphere, ideal for picking up unique items and gifts without the formality of larger shopping centers.

At Kolaportið, prices can vary greatly depending on what you're buying. While some items are priced fairly close to what you'd expect in a typical retail store, other products, especially used or vintage goods, may be priced lower. Bargaining, however, is not a common practice in Iceland. Most vendors set their prices and expect customers to pay the marked amount. That being said, in places like Kolaportið where you're dealing with individuals rather than larger businesses, there might be some room for negotiation, particularly if you're purchasing multiple items. However, it's important to approach bargaining in a respectful and polite manner. Rather than aggressively haggling, it's more about kindly asking if there's any flexibility on the price. Vendors are more likely to offer a small discount if you show genuine interest in their products and are friendly in your approach.

Another tip for shopping in local markets is to pay attention to the types of products that are uniquely Icelandic. For example, many vendors at markets sell handmade woolen goods such as scarves, sweaters, and mittens, all crafted from Icelandic wool, which is known for its warmth and durability. The traditional **lopapeysa**, a hand-knit sweater with a circular yoke pattern, is particularly popular and makes for an iconic Icelandic souvenir. However, these items can sometimes be expensive, as they are handmade and of high quality. When considering whether to buy such an item, it's important to appreciate the craftsmanship and the fact that these products are typically made by local artisans, not mass-produced. Though you may be able to find similar-looking items in larger stores or tourist shops, buying directly from the market ensures you're supporting local craftspeople and often getting a higher quality product.

For tourists visiting outside of Reykjavík, local markets can often be found in smaller towns and villages, especially during festivals and special events. These markets are a great way to interact with Icelanders in a more intimate setting and to find products that reflect the particular character of that region. For example, in towns like **Akureyri** or **Egilsstaðir**, local markets are often focused on handmade goods such as pottery, jewelry, or woodworking, as well as local food products like cheeses, jams, and smoked fish. In these smaller markets, bargaining is generally not expected, and prices are typically set. However, just like in the larger markets, showing interest and engaging in friendly conversation with vendors can sometimes lead to small discounts or special offers.

When shopping for local foods at markets, one of the highlights for tourists is the chance to sample some of Iceland's more unusual delicacies. Items like **hákarla**, the famous fermented shark, or **harðfiskur**, dried fish, may not be to everyone's taste, but they offer a glimpse into Iceland's culinary traditions. Some vendors may offer samples, which is a great way to try something new before committing to a purchase. Additionally, local markets often sell products made from Iceland's natural resources, such as **seaweed** and **lava salt**, which make for interesting souvenirs and gifts.

While Iceland is not generally known for a culture of haggling, there are still ways to save money when shopping in markets. For example, shopping at the end of the day, just before a market closes, can sometimes result in discounts, as vendors may prefer to sell their goods at a lower price rather than packing them up. Additionally, buying in bulk or purchasing multiple items from the same vendor can sometimes lead to a better deal. If you're polite and friendly, vendors may be willing to round down the total cost or offer a small discount as a gesture of goodwill.

Another thing to keep in mind when shopping in Icelandic markets is that credit cards are widely accepted throughout the country, even in smaller markets and among individual vendors. This makes it easy for tourists to shop without worrying about carrying large amounts of cash. However, it's always a good idea to have some cash on hand, especially when visiting markets in more remote areas where card payments may not be as common. The Icelandic currency is the **Icelandic króna** (ISK), and while exchange rates can vary, it's helpful to familiarize yourself with the value of the króna before heading to the markets, so you have a sense of how much you're spending.

For those looking for other markets beyond Kolaportið, the **Farmers Market Reykjavík** offers a wonderful selection of locally produced goods with an emphasis on sustainability and traditional Icelandic craftsmanship. Unlike Kolaportið, this market is more focused on high-quality products and contemporary Icelandic design. Here, visitors can find a range of fashion items, home décor, and accessories, often crafted from natural materials like wool and leather. The Farmers Market is a great place for tourists who want to purchase something uniquely Icelandic but with a modern twist.

In addition to physical markets, Iceland is home to various craft fairs and pop-up markets that take place during special events and holidays. For example, around Christmas, Reykjavík and other towns host **Christmas markets**, where visitors can buy handmade ornaments, holiday decorations, and other seasonal goods. These markets often have a festive atmosphere, with live music, food stalls, and opportunities to meet local artisans. If you're visiting Iceland during the holiday season, these markets are a great way to find unique gifts while experiencing the Icelandic take on Christmas traditions.

CHAPTER 13

PHOTOGRAPHY, ARTS, AND NATURE

Local Wildlife and Nature Reserves

Iceland is not just known for its dramatic landscapes and natural beauty but also for its rich wildlife and numerous nature reserves, which are a significant draw for tourists. The country's unique location and climate have created a diverse ecosystem, with a variety of birds, marine life, and land animals that can't be found anywhere else in the world. Nature reserves across the country serve as protected areas where tourists can look around Iceland's wildlife while preserving the delicate balance of its ecosystem.

One of the most famous and easily recognizable birds in Iceland is the **Atlantic puffin**. These small, colorful birds are a favorite among tourists, thanks to their distinctive beaks and comical waddle. Puffins can be found in large colonies along the coast during their breeding season, which lasts from May to August. Some of the best places to see puffins in Iceland are along the southern coast, particularly in **Vestmannaeyjar (the Westman Islands)**, where the largest puffin colony in the world resides. Additionally, the cliffs at **Dyrhólaey** and **Látrabjarg** in the Westfjords are also excellent spots for puffin watching. Visitors should note that puffins nest in burrows along cliff edges, so it's essential to approach carefully and avoid disturbing the birds. Guided tours are available for tourists who want to get up close to these fascinating creatures without harming their habitat.

While puffins are one of the most popular bird species in Iceland, the country is also home to a variety of other birds, making it a paradise for birdwatchers. One of the most significant birdwatching sites in Iceland is **Lake Mývatn**, located in the north of the country. This shallow lake and its surrounding wetlands are home to over 115 species of birds, including several species of ducks, geese, and swans. The **Great Northern Diver**, known for its haunting calls, can also be found here, along with the **Gyrfalcon**, Iceland's national bird. The diversity of birdlife around Lake Mývatn is due to the nutrient-rich waters, which support an abundance of insect life, providing a crucial food source for the birds. For tourists, visiting Lake Mývatn offers not only the chance to see rare bird species but also to look around one of Iceland's most geologically fascinating regions, with its volcanic craters, lava fields, and hot springs.

Beyond birdlife, Iceland's waters are home to some of the most majestic creatures on earth: whales. Whale watching is one of the most popular activities for tourists visiting Iceland, and several regions offer excellent opportunities to see these giants of the sea. **Húsavík**, a small town in the north, is often referred to as the whale-watching capital of Iceland, and it's one of the best places in the world to see a variety of whale species, including **humpback whales, minke whales**, and sometimes even the elusive **blue whale**. Whale-watching tours are available from several towns, including Reykjavík, **Akureyri**, and **Reykjavík's Old Harbor**, and many of these tours have a high success rate for whale sightings. The best time for whale watching is from April to October, when the whales migrate to the nutrient-rich waters around Iceland to feed. Seeing a whale breach the water's surface or witnessing a pod of dolphins swimming alongside a boat is a once-in-a-lifetime experience that brings many tourists back to Iceland year after year.

In addition to whales, Iceland's waters are also home to a variety of other marine life, including **seals**. Seals are often spotted along Iceland's coast, particularly in the **Jökulsárlón glacier lagoon**, where they can be seen swimming among the icebergs. Seal colonies can also be found around the **Vatnsnes Peninsula**, where the **Hvítserkur rock formation** is a popular spot for seal watching. These playful animals often bask on the rocks or swim close to shore, making them easy to observe from a distance. Several tour operators offer seal-watching excursions, and some even provide the opportunity to go snorkeling or diving with the seals for a closer look at these curious creatures.

For those interested in exploring Iceland's natural habitats, the country's many nature reserves provide a sanctuary for both wildlife and visitors. One of the most famous nature reserves in Iceland is **Þingvellir National Park**, a UNESCO World Heritage site that is not only rich in history but also in wildlife. Located on the boundary between the Eurasian and North American tectonic plates, Þingvellir is home to a variety of bird species, including ducks, geese, and swans, as well as Arctic foxes, which are Iceland's only native land mammal. The park's lakes and rivers are also home to several species of fish, including the **Arctic char** and **brown trout**, making it a popular destination for fishing enthusiasts. Þingvellir's diverse landscape, which includes rift valleys, waterfalls, and lava fields, provides a unique habitat for Iceland's wildlife and offers visitors the chance to see animals in their natural environment.

Another important nature reserve is the **Vatnajökull National Park**, which covers over 14,000 square kilometers and includes Europe's largest glacier, **Vatnajökull**. This vast park is home to a variety of wildlife, including reindeer, which were introduced to Iceland in the 18th century and now roam the eastern part of the country. The park's glaciers and rivers are also home to several species of birds, including the **pink-footed goose** and the **great skua**, a large seabird known for its aggressive behavior when defending its territory. For tourists, Vatnajökull National Park offers a wealth of outdoor activities, including glacier hiking, ice climbing, and bird watching. The park's remote and rugged terrain provides a glimpse into the raw, untouched beauty of Iceland's wilderness, making it a must-visit destination for nature lovers.

In the Westfjords, **Hornstrandir Nature Reserve** is one of the most remote and untouched areas of Iceland. This wilderness area, which is accessible only by boat, is home to a large population of Arctic foxes, as well as several species of seabirds, including puffins, guillemots, and razorbills. The Arctic fox is Iceland's only native mammal, and Hornstrandir offers one of the best chances to see these elusive animals in the wild. The foxes are known for their curious and playful nature, and visitors to the reserve may be lucky enough to see them up close. Hornstrandir's rugged cliffs and dramatic coastline also provide excellent opportunities for birdwatching, with colonies of seabirds nesting along the cliffs. For tourists seeking an off-the-beaten-path adventure, a visit to Hornstrandir is a chance to experience Iceland's wildlife in one of the most remote and pristine environments in the country.

For visitors interested in learning more about Iceland's wildlife and conservation efforts, several organizations and centers around the country focus on preserving the natural environment and educating the public. The **Seal Center** in **Hvammstangi** offers exhibitions on Iceland's seal populations and their habitats, as well as information on conservation efforts to protect these animals. The center also organizes seal-watching tours and research trips, giving visitors the opportunity to learn more about these fascinating creatures. Similarly, the **Whale Museum** in Húsavík provides an in-depth look at the various whale species that inhabit Icelandic waters, as well as the history of whaling in Iceland and current conservation efforts.

Iceland's wildlife and nature reserves are a vital part of the country's identity, offering tourists a chance to connect with nature in a way that is both educational and awe-inspiring. Whether you're watching puffins nest on a cliffside, spotting whales from a boat, or exploring the remote wilderness of a national park, Iceland's wildlife experiences are unforgettable. The country's commitment to preserving its natural habitats and protecting its wildlife ensures that these experiences will continue to be available for future generations of tourists. For visitors, respecting the environment and observing wildlife responsibly is crucial to maintaining the delicate balance of Iceland's ecosystems, ensuring that the country's natural wonders remain untouched for years to come.

Photography Tips and Best Spots

Iceland is a dream destination for photographers, with its vast and diverse landscapes offering endless opportunities for capturing stunning images. From volcanic craters and glaciers to black sand beaches and towering waterfalls, the country provides a variety of natural backdrops that are perfect for both professional photographers and hobbyists alike. Whether you're photographing the vibrant colors of the Northern Lights or the peaceful beauty of the Icelandic countryside, having a few photography tips in mind can make a world of difference in capturing the best possible shots. Knowing where to go and how to approach the country's unique scenery is essential for making the most of your time in Iceland.

One of the most iconic subjects for photographers in Iceland is its **waterfalls**, which are scattered across the country and offer breathtaking scenes to capture. Among the most famous is **Seljalandsfoss**, located along the southern coast, which is unique because you can walk behind the waterfall and photograph it from multiple angles. The falling water framed by the surrounding cliffs, especially at sunset, creates an almost magical effect, making it one of the most photographed spots in the country. A tripod is essential here to capture the best long-exposure shots, which allow you to blur the motion of the water and create a silky, smooth effect.

It's also advisable to bring a lens cloth, as the spray from the waterfall can quickly cover your camera lens. Nearby, the towering **Skógafoss** waterfall also provides incredible photographic opportunities. With its powerful stream and mist rising into the air, Skógafoss is best captured from the base, where you can showcase its sheer size and strength, or from the top, where you can capture the landscape that stretches out behind it.

For photographers interested in more dramatic landscapes, **Reynisfjara** beach on the southern coast offers a stunning contrast between the black volcanic sand and the white waves crashing against the shore. This beach is known for its **basalt columns**, which rise up like natural sculptures, and the **Reynisdrangar sea stacks**, which can be seen jutting out of the ocean just offshore. These unique rock formations make for great focal points in landscape photography, and the dark, moody atmosphere of the beach lends itself well to creative compositions. However, visitors should be cautious when photographing here, as the waves at Reynisfjara can be unpredictable and dangerous. It's important to keep a safe distance from the water and remain aware of the tide while taking photos.

Another popular destination for photographers is **Jökulsárlón**, a glacial lagoon in southeastern Iceland. Here, large chunks of ice break off from the Vatnajökull glacier and float in the lagoon, creating a surreal, ever-changing landscape of icebergs in shades of blue and white. Photographers can capture the contrast between the calm, still water of the lagoon and the rugged, icy shapes floating within it. On the nearby **Diamond Beach**, these icebergs often wash up on shore, where they glisten like gemstones against the black sand, making for striking and unusual photographs. Jökulsárlón is especially photogenic at sunrise and sunset, when the light creates soft reflections on the water and enhances the color of the ice. For capturing this scene, a wide-angle lens is ideal for fitting the entire landscape into the frame, while a polarizing filter can help reduce glare and enhance the colors of the ice.

Of course, no photography trip to Iceland would be complete without trying to capture the **Northern Lights**, or **Aurora Borealis**, which are one of the most sought-after subjects for photographers visiting the country. The Northern Lights are most visible during the winter months, from September to March, when the nights are long and dark. To photograph the aurora, it's important to find a location far from any light pollution, such as in the countryside or near smaller towns. Some of the best places for Northern Lights photography include **Þingvellir National Park, Kirkjufell Mountain**, and the **Westfjords**. The key to photographing the Northern Lights is using a long exposure to capture the light as it dances across the sky. A tripod is essential for this, as it keeps the camera steady during the long exposure. Set your camera to a high ISO setting (usually between 800 and 3200), use a wide aperture (around $f/2.8$ to $f/4$), and experiment with exposure times (typically between 10 and 30 seconds) to get the best results.

For photographers interested in capturing Iceland's wildlife, the country offers several opportunities to photograph native species in their natural habitats. **Puffins**, with their bright orange beaks and charming expressions, are a favorite subject for wildlife photographers. During the summer months, puffins nest in large colonies along Iceland's cliffs, with some of the best spots for puffin photography located in **Vestmannaeyjar**, **Dyrhólaey**, and **Látrabjarg**. Puffins are relatively easy to approach, making them excellent subjects for close-up shots, but it's important to respect their space and avoid disturbing their nests. A zoom lens is helpful for capturing detailed images of the birds without getting too close.

In addition to its landscapes and wildlife, Iceland's unique **geothermal features** provide another fantastic opportunity for photography. The geothermal areas around **Geysir** and **Strokkur** in the **Golden Circle** are among the most well-known, with Strokkur regularly erupting every few minutes, sending a column of boiling water into the air. Capturing the moment just before or during an eruption can result in dynamic and exciting photographs. Patience and timing are key here, as you may need to wait for the right moment to get the shot. Wide-angle lenses are ideal for capturing the geyser's eruption against the backdrop of the surrounding landscape, and using a fast shutter speed can help freeze the action as the water shoots skyward.

When photographing Iceland's landscapes, it's essential to be aware of the changing weather conditions. Iceland is known for its unpredictable weather, and photographers should always be prepared for rain, wind, and sudden changes in light. Having the right gear, such as a waterproof camera cover and sturdy tripod, can make a big difference in ensuring that you can continue photographing even in challenging conditions. Layering your clothing is also crucial, as temperatures can drop quickly, especially in the highlands or near glaciers. Always keep a spare set of batteries with you, as cold weather can drain batteries faster than usual.

Another tip for capturing Iceland's best photography spots is to avoid peak tourist times. Some of Iceland's most popular sites, such as **Gullfoss** and **Seljalandsfoss**, can get crowded during the middle of the day, especially in the summer months when tourism is at its peak. To avoid crowds and get more serene shots, it's best to visit these locations early in the morning or later in the evening when the light is softer and there are fewer people around. This not only makes for better photos but also allows you to enjoy the landscape without the distractions of large groups of tourists.

For more adventurous photographers, Iceland's **highlands** offer some of the most remote and untouched landscapes in the country. Areas like **Landmannalaugar** and the **Þórsmörk Valley** are famous for their colorful rhyolite mountains, vast lava fields, and rugged terrain. Hiking through these regions allows photographers to capture truly otherworldly landscapes that feel far removed from the more accessible parts of the country. However, visiting the highlands requires a four-wheel-drive vehicle, and it's essential to check road conditions and weather forecasts before heading out, as these areas can be difficult to access during certain times of the year.

Finally, for those looking to capture a different perspective on Iceland's landscapes, **drone photography** has become increasingly popular in recent years. Using a drone allows photographers to get aerial shots of the country's waterfalls, glaciers, and volcanic craters, offering a bird's-eye view that showcases the scale and beauty of Iceland's natural wonders. However, it's important to note that there are restrictions on drone use in certain areas, especially near national parks and sensitive wildlife habitats. Always check local regulations and guidelines before flying a drone, and be respectful of the environment and other visitors.

Photography and Drone Regulations

When visiting Iceland, one of the most popular activities for tourists is capturing its stunning landscapes through photography. The country's natural beauty, from its vast glaciers and black sand beaches to the iconic Northern Lights, makes it a paradise for photographers. However, it's important for tourists to be aware of the regulations surrounding both photography and drone use to ensure they capture the best shots without violating any rules or disturbing the environment.

Photography in public spaces in Iceland is generally permitted and doesn't require any special permissions. Visitors are free to photograph landscapes, wildlife, and most public places without restrictions. However, when it comes to photographing people, the same general rule of respecting privacy applies as it does anywhere else. While Icelanders are generally welcoming and friendly, it's polite to ask for permission if you're photographing individuals, especially in more personal settings like markets or small gatherings. It's also important to remember that while most public spaces are free to photograph, certain cultural and historic sites may have their own rules regarding photography, especially in places like churches or museums.

In some areas, particularly those with large crowds or fragile environments, there may be designated zones where photography is restricted. Þingvellir National Park, for instance, is a UNESCO World Heritage Site, and while photography is allowed, there are specific areas where the use of certain equipment, like tripods or large camera setups, might be limited to avoid damage to the site or inconvenience to other visitors. Similarly, at places like Jökulsárlón Glacier Lagoon or Geysir, it's essential to respect the boundaries and paths set up to protect the environment. Venturing off designated paths to get a better shot can cause harm to the landscape, especially in sensitive geothermal areas where the ground is fragile.

One aspect of photography that has gained increasing popularity in Iceland is the use of drones. Aerial photography with drones allows tourists to capture Iceland's landscapes from entirely new perspectives, showcasing the vastness of its glaciers, volcanoes, and coastline. However, Iceland has strict regulations regarding drone use, and these rules are in place to protect both the environment and the safety and privacy of people.

If you plan to fly a drone in Iceland, it's crucial to familiarize yourself with the country's drone regulations before you take off. First and foremost, drone operators must adhere to the Icelandic Transport Authority's rules for unmanned aerial vehicles (UAVs). According to these regulations, drones must not be flown above 120 meters (400 feet) in altitude and must always remain within the operator's line of sight. This is to ensure that drones do not interfere with manned aircraft, which may be flying at low altitudes, especially in rural or wilderness areas where sightseeing flights or search and rescue missions might be taking place.

It's also important to note that drones should not be flown near airports, heliports, or landing areas used by aircraft. There are specific no-fly zones around airports such as Keflavík International Airport, Reykjavík Domestic Airport, and smaller regional airports like Akureyri and Egilsstaðir. Flying a drone near these areas can pose serious risks to aviation safety and result in heavy fines. Additionally, drones are not allowed in built-up areas or close to large crowds without special permission from the Icelandic authorities. This means that flying a drone in Reykjavík's city center, for instance, is prohibited unless you have received explicit permission from the relevant local authorities.

In popular tourist destinations, there are additional restrictions on drone use to protect both the environment and the visitor experience. In national parks like Vatnajökull, Þingvellir, and Snæfellsjökull, drones are generally prohibited to avoid disturbing the wildlife and other visitors. These parks are some of the most visited sites in Iceland, and the sound of drones can detract from the natural peace and serenity that people come to experience. While it may be tempting to get a sweeping aerial shot of these iconic locations, it's essential to respect the rules in place to preserve these areas for future visitors.

Drone users should also be aware of restrictions in locations that are considered sacred or culturally significant. For example, flying a drone near churches, cemeteries, or ancient historical sites is typically not allowed without permission. In Iceland, many such sites hold deep cultural importance, and the sound of drones can be seen as disruptive or disrespectful. If you're unsure whether drone use is permitted in a particular area, it's best to check with local authorities or guides before launching your drone.

In addition to the specific legal restrictions, it's important for drone operators to consider the impact their activity may have on Iceland's wildlife. Iceland is home to several species of birds, including the famous Atlantic puffin, as well as other animals like seals and reindeer. The sound and presence of drones can cause significant stress to wildlife, especially during breeding seasons. For example, in areas where puffins nest along cliffs, drones can scare the birds, potentially causing them to abandon their nests. This can have devastating effects on bird populations, so it's crucial to avoid flying drones near nesting areas or wildlife reserves.

To fly a drone in Iceland legally, drones weighing more than 250 grams must be registered with the Icelandic Transport Authority. Operators are also required to carry liability insurance for any damage their drone may cause. This insurance is necessary because accidents can happen, and a drone that crashes into property or injures someone can result in legal and financial consequences. If you're renting a drone in Iceland, the rental company may provide insurance, but it's always a good idea to check the details before flying.

One important aspect of drone photography that many visitors may not be aware of is the need to respect the privacy of others. While it's exciting to capture aerial shots of Iceland's landscapes, it's essential to avoid flying drones over private property or near homes without permission. Iceland has strict privacy laws, and using a drone to capture footage in areas where people expect privacy, such as private residences or personal gatherings, can result in legal action.

When it comes to night photography, drones equipped with lights may seem like a great tool for capturing unique perspectives of Iceland's iconic Northern Lights. However, flying drones at night is generally not recommended, as it increases the risk of losing control of the drone or colliding with objects. Additionally, the lights on a drone can interfere with the long-exposure photography that many visitors use to capture the auroras, diminishing the experience for others.

For those who are new to drone photography or unfamiliar with Iceland's drone regulations, it's highly recommended to join a guided drone photography tour. Several tour operators offer specialized trips that cater to drone enthusiasts, providing both the knowledge and the necessary permissions to fly drones in stunning yet regulated areas. These tours often include lessons on drone operation and safety, as well as tips for capturing the best aerial shots of Iceland's landscapes.

Aside from drones, photography in Iceland also requires an awareness of Leave No Trace principles. Iceland's landscapes are fragile, and in recent years, the increase in tourism has put significant pressure on the environment. When setting up your camera or drone for the perfect shot, it's important to stay on marked paths and avoid trampling on vegetation or disturbing natural features. Iceland's moss-covered lava fields, for instance, take centuries to grow, and walking off-trail can cause irreversible damage. Respecting these guidelines ensures that future generations can continue to enjoy Iceland's natural beauty.

CHAPTER 14

EXTRA INFORMATION FOR TOURISTS

Public Wi-Fi Availability

Public Wi-Fi availability in Iceland is something that tourists will find quite reliable and accessible, especially in urban areas and popular tourist destinations. Iceland has made considerable strides in providing internet access to its residents and visitors alike.

In the larger cities and towns, such as Reykjavík, Akureyri, and Keflavík, Wi-Fi is widely available in public spaces. Many of the cafés, restaurants, and bars offer free Wi-Fi to their customers, making it easy for tourists to sit down, relax, and use the internet while enjoying a meal or coffee. For example, in Reykjavík, nearly every café or coffee shop provides Wi-Fi without the need for a password, and the service is typically free. It's quite common for tourists to use these spots to check their emails, upload photos, or even plan their next steps. The Wi-Fi in these places tends to be of good quality and fast enough to handle most tasks, including video calls or streaming.

If you're staying at a hotel or guesthouse, you'll likely have access to Wi-Fi in your room or in common areas. Most hotels in Iceland provide free Wi-Fi for guests, and the signal quality is generally strong enough for streaming, video conferencing, and other bandwidth-heavy activities. In rural areas, even some remote lodges and guesthouses offer Wi-Fi, although the speed may not always be as fast as what you're used to in cities. However, for basic browsing and staying connected, it should suffice.

For travelers moving between locations, Wi-Fi is often available at transportation hubs, such as airports and bus stations. Keflavík International Airport, the main gateway for international tourists, provides free Wi-Fi to all passengers. Upon arriving in Iceland or while waiting for a departing flight, you can easily connect to the airport's Wi-Fi without any hassle. This service is quite reliable, allowing travelers to download maps, check into flights, or arrange transportation once they land. Major bus terminals, such as the BSÍ bus terminal in Reykjavík, also offer Wi-Fi, making it convenient for tourists to plan their next move while waiting for public transport.

When it comes to public transportation, however, the availability of Wi-Fi is not as widespread as in some other countries. Iceland's public buses, especially in Reykjavík, do not generally offer Wi-Fi on board. If you're relying on public transportation for travel within cities, it's advisable to use mobile data or download offline maps before starting your trip, as Wi-Fi may not be available on the buses themselves. However, some of the longer-distance buses, particularly those operated by tour companies for popular routes like the Golden Circle or trips to Jökulsárlón, may offer Wi-Fi. It's worth checking with the tour operator in advance to see if this is included.

For those driving through Iceland or exploring more remote areas, access to public Wi-Fi can be more limited. In the highlands or along less-traveled roads, Wi-Fi might not be available at all, and relying on mobile data may be necessary. Fortunately, Iceland has an excellent mobile network, and purchasing a local SIM card can be a good option for travelers who need internet access in more rural areas. Many convenience stores, gas stations, and supermarkets sell SIM cards with data plans, and the process of setting up mobile internet is usually quick and easy. The major telecom providers, such as Siminn, Vodafone, and Nova, offer good coverage across most of the country, although there may be some dead zones in the more remote regions.

In some cases, free Wi-Fi is available at public locations like libraries and museums. For example, in Reykjavík, the Reykjavík City Library provides free Wi-Fi to visitors, making it a quiet spot for tourists who need to work or catch up on emails. Many museums, including the National Museum of Iceland, also offer free Wi-Fi, allowing visitors to access additional information about exhibits or share their experiences online while exploring. While visiting such places, you can take advantage of the complimentary internet to make your experience more interactive and informed.

In addition to public Wi-Fi, many tourist attractions in Iceland, particularly those in more popular areas, are equipped with free or paid Wi-Fi services. For example, Blue

Lagoon, one of the most visited tourist spots in Iceland, provides Wi-Fi throughout the entire complex. This means that while you're relaxing in the geothermal waters, you can still stay connected, whether to check emails or post about your visit. Similarly, places like the Golden Circle attractions—Gullfoss, Geysir, and Þingvellir National Park—usually have visitor centers where you can access Wi-Fi.

One of the most convenient ways to ensure reliable internet access throughout your trip is to rent a portable Wi-Fi device, also known as a pocket Wi-Fi. Several companies in Iceland offer this service, allowing tourists to rent a small device that creates a personal Wi-Fi hotspot. These devices can be rented at the airport, through car rental agencies, or booked online before arriving in Iceland. Portable Wi-Fi is a particularly good option for those who plan to travel to more remote areas where public Wi-Fi may not be available. With a portable Wi-Fi device, you can have internet access wherever you go, as long as there's mobile network coverage. This is ideal for those on road trips, camping, or hiking in more isolated parts of the country.

If you choose not to rely on Wi-Fi and prefer mobile data, as mentioned earlier, purchasing a local SIM card is a practical solution. SIM cards in Iceland come with various data packages, so you can choose the amount of data that suits your needs. Prices are generally reasonable, and you can purchase cards with pre-loaded data at convenience stores or directly from the telecom providers. This is a particularly useful option for travelers who need constant access to maps, navigation apps, or communication tools while on the go.

It's also important to be mindful of your online security when using public Wi-Fi, especially in busy areas like airports or cafés. While Iceland is generally a safe country, it's still possible for hackers to exploit unsecured networks. It's a good idea to avoid accessing sensitive information, such as bank accounts or personal emails, when using public Wi-Fi. Instead, use secure websites with HTTPS encryption and consider using a virtual private network (VPN) to protect your data when using open networks.

For those who prefer to keep up with work or need faster, more reliable internet connections during their trip, there are co-working spaces available in Reykjavík and other major towns. Co-working spaces, such as Kaffi Vinyl and The Co-Working Hub in Reykjavík, provide tourists and digital nomads with reliable internet, quiet working conditions, and comfortable seating areas. These spaces often offer a more stable internet connection than typical public Wi-Fi, making them ideal for remote work, uploading large files, or simply having uninterrupted access to the web.

Local Guides and Tour Companies

When visiting Iceland, relying on local guides and tour companies can significantly enhance your travel experience. Iceland is a country full of natural beauty, with landscapes ranging from volcanic craters and glaciers to geothermal hot springs and thundering waterfalls. Navigating such diverse terrain can be challenging for tourists, especially if you're unfamiliar with the country's geography or weather conditions.

Many local guides in Iceland have grown up with the land, and their intimate knowledge of the environment, folklore, and traditions adds an extra layer of depth to any tour. These guides can take you to hidden gems and remote locations that you might miss if traveling on your own. Whether you're exploring Iceland's highlands, hunting for the Northern Lights, or trekking across glaciers, local guides are often well-equipped to offer you a safe and enjoyable experience. Moreover, many of the tour companies operating in Iceland are dedicated to sustainable tourism, meaning they prioritize preserving the environment and supporting local communities.

Iceland has a wide variety of tour companies offering trips that cater to all types of travelers. If you're looking for an all-inclusive experience, larger companies such as Gray Line Iceland, Reykjavik Excursions, and Iceland Travel offer comprehensive tours that cover many of the country's major attractions. These companies typically provide transportation, guides, and sometimes even meals, making them a convenient choice for those who prefer a structured travel experience. Their tours often include stops at popular destinations like the Golden Circle, Blue Lagoon, and South Coast, ensuring you get to see Iceland's most iconic sights. These companies also offer a variety of options for different budgets and time frames, so whether you're visiting for just a few days or a couple of weeks, you can find a tour that fits your schedule.

For more adventurous travelers, there are numerous tour companies specializing in specific activities such as glacier hiking, ice climbing, or snowmobiling. One such company is Arcanum Glacier Tours, which offers trips onto the Mýrdalsjökull glacier, where participants can look around ice caves, crevasses, and stunning ice formations. Their experienced guides ensure that you're well-equipped and safe while traversing the icy terrain. Similarly, Arctic Adventures provides a range of adventure-focused tours, from river rafting and snorkeling between tectonic plates at Silfra to multi-day trekking tours through Iceland's highlands.

One of the most sought-after experiences in Iceland is witnessing the Northern Lights, and several local tour companies specialize in Northern Lights hunting. Superjeep.is, for example, takes tourists on off-road adventures in rugged Super Jeeps to chase the auroras in areas with little to no light pollution. These tours often take you far from the city, into remote regions where the Northern Lights are more visible, increasing your chances of catching the display. The guides are highly knowledgeable about weather patterns and aurora activity, using their expertise to track the best locations for viewing.

In addition to adventure tours, Iceland also offers more niche experiences through smaller, specialized tour companies. If you're interested in Icelandic history and culture, Saga Travel offers historical tours that delve into the country's Viking past and its unique folklore. These tours often include visits to historical sites, such as Þingvellir National Park, where the world's first parliament was established, and Reykholt, the home of the famous medieval chieftain and historian Snorri Sturluson. By choosing a specialized tour, you can dive deeper into Iceland's rich cultural heritage, learning stories and legends that go beyond the typical tourist experience.

Another unique offering comes from GeoIceland, which focuses on the geological wonders of Iceland. Their tours are designed for travelers who want to learn about the volcanic and tectonic activity that has shaped the country's landscape over millions of years. They take tourists to areas like Hekla, one of Iceland's most active volcanoes, and Askja, a caldera in the central highlands known for its lunar-like landscape. For geology enthusiasts, these tours provide a fascinating look at Iceland's natural history, offering detailed explanations of volcanic eruptions, glaciers, and geothermal features.

If you prefer smaller, more intimate tour experiences, there are plenty of companies that cater to private or small-group tours. Hidden Iceland is a boutique tour operator that offers personalized itineraries for travelers who want to avoid the crowds and look around more off-the-beaten-path locations. Their guides work closely with you to create a customized experience based on your interests, whether that's hiking through untouched wilderness, exploring remote fjords, or visiting lesser-known waterfalls. Private tours like these allow for a more flexible and personal experience, as you can set the pace and focus on the aspects of Iceland that interest you most.

When it comes to booking local guides or tours, the process is fairly straightforward, and there are multiple ways to go about it. Most companies offer online booking through their websites, where you can choose your tour, specify dates, and make payments in advance. For those who prefer to plan as they go, many tour operators have offices in Reykjavík or other major towns, where you can book tours in person. Some hotels and guesthouses also partner with local tour companies and can help arrange tours for you directly, offering recommendations based on your preferences and availability.

It's important to note that Iceland's weather can be unpredictable, especially during the winter months, and some tours may be subject to cancellations due to poor conditions. However, reputable tour companies always prioritize safety and will offer alternatives or reschedule if conditions are unsafe for travel. This is another reason why booking through experienced local guides is advantageous—they are familiar with the terrain and weather patterns and can make informed decisions to keep you safe.

Many local guides in Iceland are also certified in wilderness first aid and have extensive knowledge of rescue techniques, which is especially important for those venturing into remote areas or participating in activities like glacier hiking or snowmobiling. Their expertise not only enhances the safety of the tours but also ensures that participants can enjoy their activities with peace of mind, knowing they are in capable hands.

Lastly, for travelers who are conscious of their environmental impact, Iceland has several tour companies that emphasize eco-friendly and sustainable travel practices. Iceland Eco Tours, for example, focuses on minimizing their environmental footprint by promoting sustainable tourism. Their tours are designed to reduce impact on the land, and they work closely with local communities to support responsible travel. By choosing a tour operator that prioritizes sustainability, tourists can contribute to the preservation of Iceland's natural beauty and cultural heritage while enjoying their travel experiences.

Operator Guide

When visiting Iceland, having access to a reliable operator guide can make a huge difference in how smoothly your trip goes. Iceland is a country known for its rugged landscapes, unpredictable weather, and remote locations, so it is crucial to understand how to interact with the various tour operators and transportation services in the country. Whether you're planning an adventure tour, arranging local transportation, or simply seeking advice on the best ways to look around, working with the right operators can elevate your experience and ensure your time in Iceland is enjoyable, safe, and memorable.

Iceland's tourism sector is well-organized, with a number of operators specializing in everything from guided hikes to sightseeing tours, Northern Lights expeditions, and transportation services. Because of the country's unique geography, it's essential to rely on operators that know the terrain well and can provide valuable insights. Many operators in Iceland focus on sustainability and eco-tourism, aiming to preserve the natural beauty of the land while still offering immersive experiences for visitors.

One of the first things to understand when navigating the various operators in Iceland is that the quality of service is typically high, with most companies putting a strong emphasis on safety and professionalism. Icelandic tour guides are well-trained, and many have certifications in wilderness safety, first aid, and glacier travel, ensuring that tourists are in safe hands when engaging in potentially risky activities like hiking or exploring remote areas. This is especially important in Iceland, where weather conditions can change rapidly and certain terrains, like glaciers, can be hazardous without proper expertise.

For tourists who want to experience Iceland's natural beauty without taking on the responsibility of navigating unfamiliar landscapes, operator services like Gray Line Iceland or Reykjavik Excursions offer a wide range of options. These larger operators provide scheduled tours to Iceland's most popular destinations, such as the Golden Circle, South Coast, Snæfellsnes Peninsula, and Blue Lagoon. What makes these operators particularly appealing is the ease of access—they offer pick-up and drop-off services in major areas like Reykjavík, which means travelers don't have to worry about renting a car or figuring out how to get from one place to another.

If you're looking to get off the beaten path, smaller operators often provide more tailored and specialized services. Companies like Hidden Iceland or Icelandic Mountain Guides offer bespoke tours that cater to specific interests, such as glacier walks, ice cave explorations, and even helicopter tours over volcanic regions. These smaller operators focus on delivering a more personalized experience, taking visitors to less-crowded areas while providing deep insight into the local culture and environment. Their guides are often locals who have grown up exploring Iceland's remote regions and can share knowledge that goes beyond what's typically covered in guidebooks.

Another vital role that operators play in Iceland is ensuring safe travel across the country's sometimes challenging roads. Iceland is famous for its Ring Road, a highway that circles the island and provides access to most of the country's major attractions. However, many of Iceland's most scenic spots lie off the main road, accessible only via rough gravel paths or F-roads, which are mountain roads that require four-wheel-drive vehicles to find your way. If you're unfamiliar with driving in these conditions, renting a car with a specialized operator can be essential. Companies like Sadcars or Blue Car Rental provide vehicles that are specifically suited for Iceland's terrain, along with advice on how to safely travel through the highlands or remote regions.

For those interested in a more independent travel experience, Icelandic operators also offer self-drive tours where the itinerary is pre-planned, but you have the flexibility to look around on your own. These packages usually include accommodations, car rental, and a detailed itinerary with suggested routes and stops. They can be an excellent option for visitors who want the freedom to look around at their own pace but still appreciate the convenience and local expertise provided by tour operators.

One of the most appealing aspects of Iceland's tourism industry is the wide range of adventure sports and outdoor activities available, and there are several operators that cater specifically to adrenaline-seekers. Arcanum Glacier Tours, for example, specializes in glacier hiking and snowmobiling on Mýrdalsjökull Glacier. Dive.is offers the unique experience of diving or snorkeling between tectonic plates at Silfra, located in Þingvellir National Park. These operators are well-equipped to handle the unique challenges of Iceland's landscapes, providing necessary safety gear and expert guidance.

Iceland's unpredictable weather is a constant factor, and tour operators are adept at managing the challenges it presents. Whether you are planning a Northern Lights tour or a whale-watching trip, operators often make real-time decisions based on weather conditions to ensure that you have the best possible experience. For instance, many Northern Lights tours offer a "second chance" policy, meaning that if you don't see the lights on your first attempt, you can join another tour at no extra cost on a different night. This flexibility is one of the reasons tourists find guided tours so convenient, as it takes the uncertainty out of planning in such a dynamic environment.

Public transportation in Iceland is relatively limited outside of Reykjavík, which makes operator services all the more important for those who don't want to rent a car. Operators like Straeto provide bus services in and around Reykjavík and to some of the nearby towns, but if you're planning to visit more remote areas, private transportation services provided by operators are often a better option. Some companies offer shuttle services to locations such as Jökulsárlón, Reynisfjara Black Sand Beach, and Vik for tourists who want to visit these areas without committing to a full-day tour.

For tourists who are traveling during the winter months, operators become even more critical. The weather in Iceland can be extreme, with heavy snowfall and icy roads making travel difficult for those unfamiliar with winter driving. Many tour companies offer winter-specific tours and packages that include visits to ice caves, frozen waterfalls, and other seasonal attractions. These tours are carefully curated to account for the reduced daylight hours and the potential dangers posed by winter weather, making them a safer and more enjoyable option than trying to travel independently.

In addition to traditional tours, operators in Iceland often provide specialized services for those interested in photography or other niche interests. Iceland Photo Tours, for instance, offers photography-focused trips that take tourists to some of the country's most scenic locations during optimal lighting conditions. These tours are designed for both amateur and professional photographers who want to capture Iceland's landscapes, wildlife, and Northern Lights. The guides on these tours often have extensive photography experience themselves and can offer advice on composition, settings, and techniques for capturing the perfect shot.

For eco-conscious travelers, several operators in Iceland prioritize sustainability and eco-friendly travel practices. Iceland Eco Tours is one such company, offering carbon-neutral tours that aim to minimize environmental impact while providing meaningful experiences. These tours often focus on areas of natural beauty that are not overrun with tourists, providing a more serene and eco-friendly alternative to some of the more crowded destinations.

Finally, Iceland's tour operators are increasingly focusing on accessibility, ensuring that tourists with disabilities or special needs can also enjoy the country's natural wonders. Companies like Accessible Iceland specialize in providing tours that cater to wheelchair users or those with mobility issues, offering specially adapted vehicles and routes that avoid difficult terrain. Whether it's a city tour of Reykjavík or a trip to see the Northern Lights, these operators ensure that Iceland's beauty is accessible to everyone.

HOW TO CREATE YOUR ITINERARY

Creating the perfect itinerary for a trip to Iceland is more than just listing out places to visit—it's about ensuring that every moment is well-spent, practical, and tailored to your interests. Planning the right itinerary means understanding the geography, travel times, weather conditions, and what your own expectations for the trip are. Many tourists end up overwhelmed or disappointed because they overlook the complexities involved in traveling through Iceland, where conditions can change quickly, and certain sites might be more difficult to access than anticipated. By carefully crafting a plan that takes into account your preferences, budget, and timeframe, you can ensure a smooth and satisfying travel experience that will leave you with wonderful memories.

The first step in creating your itinerary is determining your priorities. Iceland has a wide variety of attractions, and not all are accessible year-round. Think about what you want most out of your trip. Are you looking for dramatic landscapes like glaciers and volcanoes? Do you want to see the Northern Lights? Maybe you're more interested in relaxing in geothermal hot springs or exploring Icelandic culture through its museums and small towns. Defining what's most important to you will help narrow down your must-see destinations and make it easier to structure your days.

Next, consider the duration of your trip. Time is a key factor in building a successful itinerary. If you only have a few days, your focus should be on exploring a specific region rather than trying to cover too much ground. For a short stay, Reykjavík and the surrounding areas are ideal as they offer a mix of natural and cultural highlights. The famous Golden Circle route, which includes Þingvellir National Park, Geysir geothermal area, and Gullfoss waterfall, is easily accessible from the capital and can be explored in a single day. If you have a week or more, you can plan to venture further out, exploring the South Coast with its black sand beaches and towering waterfalls, or even driving the Ring Road, a full circuit around the island that showcases many of Iceland's iconic sites.

Understanding the geography of Iceland is also crucial. The country's landscapes are vast and varied, and what looks like a short distance on the map can take significantly longer due to road conditions or weather. Plan your days with realistic travel times in mind. For example, driving between Reykjavík and Jökulsárlón Glacier Lagoon takes about five hours each way. Factor in the time spent at stops along the way, like Seljalandsfoss and Skógafoss waterfalls, and you have a full day trip. Trying to cram too much into one day can lead to fatigue and prevent you from truly enjoying each location. Instead, focus on a few sites each day and give yourself ample time to explore.

It's also wise to consider the time of year when planning your itinerary. The summer months (June to August) offer the most daylight, making it easier to see more in a single day. Roads are usually clear, and nearly all sites are accessible. This is the best time to include activities like hiking, camping, and highland tours. Winter (November to February), on the other hand, presents unique challenges but also rewards, such as the opportunity to see the Northern Lights or take part in snow sports. Shorter daylight hours mean you'll need to plan carefully to fit everything in, and some areas, particularly the highlands and certain F-roads, will be off-limits. However, winter also has its own unique charm, with frozen landscapes, fewer crowds, and the chance to experience Iceland's cozy, slower-paced atmosphere.

When selecting your stops, it's helpful to categorize them into major attractions, secondary stops, and potential detours. Major attractions are the must-see places that you don't want to miss. For most people, this includes sites like the Blue Lagoon, the Golden Circle, Vatnajökull National Park, and Jökulsárlón Glacier Lagoon. Secondary stops are places you would like to see if time permits, such as smaller waterfalls, viewpoints, or lesser-known hot springs. Detours are unplanned, spontaneous stops that you might want to include if the opportunity arises—maybe a scenic viewpoint, a charming café, or a village festival you learn about along the way.

Mapping out your route is the next step. A well-planned route prevents backtracking and saves valuable time. Start by placing your must-see sites on a map and then determine the most logical order to visit them. For example, if you're starting in Reykjavík and want to see the South Coast, you would map out a route that includes Seljalandsfoss, Skógafoss, the black sand beach of Reynisfjara, and end at Jökulsárlón before looping back. If you're planning to drive the Ring Road, identify overnight stops that break up the journey into manageable segments, ensuring that you have enough daylight to drive and explore. Popular stops along the Ring Road include Akureyri in the north, Egilsstaðir in the east, and the small fishing villages along the east fjords.

Accommodations should also be factored into your itinerary early on. Because Iceland's tourism has grown rapidly in recent years, availability can be limited, particularly in remote areas. Book accommodations well in advance, especially if you're traveling during the high season or planning to stay in less populated areas. Consider the location of your lodging in relation to your planned activities for the day. Staying close to your starting point or the day's final destination reduces driving time and allows you to make the most of your day. For a more immersive experience, look for accommodations that offer unique settings, like farm stays, guesthouses in small towns, or cabins with views of the Northern Lights.

Once you have a general structure for your days, it's time to think about activities. Iceland offers a variety of options beyond sightseeing. Glacier hiking, whale watching, horseback riding, and snorkeling between tectonic plates are just a few examples. Include these in your itinerary based on your interests and physical abilities. If you're planning a more active trip, keep in mind the physical demands of certain activities and allow time to rest and recover between them. For example, if you're doing a glacier hike one day, you might want to schedule a more relaxed activity, like a hot spring visit or a scenic drive, the next day.

For travelers who want a more spontaneous experience, leaving some flexibility in your itinerary is key. While it's good to have a general plan, building in some unscheduled time allows for unexpected discoveries and changes in weather. If you find a spot you particularly enjoy, you can choose to linger without feeling pressured to move on to the next stop. On the other hand, if a site is too crowded or not as appealing as expected, you have the option to move on without disrupting the entire trip.

Don't forget to consider practical details when planning your itinerary. Fuel stations can be scarce in certain parts of Iceland, particularly in the highlands and along the eastern coast. Plan your fuel stops in advance and fill up whenever you have the opportunity, especially if you're venturing into less populated areas. Stocking up on food and supplies is also important, as restaurants and stores may not be available outside of the main towns. Having snacks, water, and emergency supplies on hand ensures you're prepared for long stretches between services.

Finally, keep in mind that Iceland's natural beauty is its biggest draw, and the best itineraries are those that leave room to appreciate it fully. Whether it's watching the sunset over a glacier, sitting by a quiet lake, or hiking to a remote waterfall, take the time to slow down and enjoy your surroundings. An itinerary should guide your travels, but it should also allow for the unexpected moments that make a trip truly memorable.

Thank you for choosing this travel guide! To help you organize your trip efficiently, we're offering a **Free Travel Planner** that you can print out and use to document your plans.

Here's how you can access and print your planner:

- **Locate the QR Code**: You'll find the QR code below this section.

- **Scan the QR Code**: Use your smartphone's camera or a QR code reader app to scan the code.

- **Download the Planner**: After scanning, you'll be directed to the download page. Follow the instructions to download the planner file.

- **Print the Planner**: Print out the planner on your home printer or at a local print shop.

- **Start Planning**: Use the printed planner to jot down your travel plans, organize your itinerary, and ensure a well-prepared trip.

CONCLUSION

As we come to the end of this guide, it's clear that Iceland offers a wealth of experiences for every type of traveler. From its striking natural landscapes, such as glaciers, volcanoes, waterfalls, and geothermal hot springs, to its rich cultural history and traditions, Iceland is a destination that captures the imagination and offers something for everyone. Whether you are someone who seeks adventure, enjoys the quiet beauty of nature, or wishes to immerse yourself in the local culture, this country provides a diverse range of activities, making it a place worth exploring in depth.

One of the key takeaways from traveling through Iceland is the unique sense of connection that the country fosters between its visitors and its environment. There is something truly special about standing on a black sand beach, watching waves crash against the shore, or walking along lava fields that have been shaped by volcanic eruptions over centuries. The vastness of the landscapes, combined with their unspoiled nature, offers a sense of peace and wonder that is hard to find elsewhere. At the same time, the small towns and villages dotted throughout Iceland give you a glimpse into local life, where tradition and modernity coexist harmoniously. The people of Iceland, with their deep respect for nature and cultural heritage, extend a warm welcome to tourists, making the experience all the more memorable.

For those planning a visit, knowing when to go and what to pack can make a big difference in how you enjoy the country. Iceland's weather, though unpredictable, is part of what makes the experience unique. Whether you're visiting in the warmer months to take in the Midnight Sun or during winter to witness the spectacular Northern Lights, each season offers its own rewards. Understanding the practical aspects of travel—such as visa requirements, local customs, transportation options, and where to stay—ensures that you're prepared to fully enjoy what Iceland has to offer. This guide has covered those important details to help you make the most of your time in the country.

Another crucial point to consider when traveling in Iceland is the importance of responsible tourism. Iceland's environment is fragile, and its landscapes are shaped by forces of nature that are as powerful as they are beautiful. Visitors are encouraged to be mindful of their impact, respecting the natural surroundings, and following local guidelines to preserve the beauty of this land for future generations. Tour operators and local guides often emphasize this, ensuring that visitors leave a minimal footprint. By supporting sustainable travel practices and engaging with local communities, tourists contribute to the ongoing efforts to protect Iceland's unique environment.

Beyond the landscapes, Iceland's culture is equally fascinating. The country's sagas, myths, and folklore are woven into the fabric of daily life, with stories of elves, trolls, and Vikings that capture the imagination. Festivals and celebrations throughout the year provide an opportunity to witness these traditions in action, from the vibrant celebrations of Þorrablót to the quieter cultural performances that showcase Icelandic music, theater, and art. Learning a few key Icelandic phrases or engaging with local customs will help enrich your interactions with the people and give you a deeper appreciation for the culture.

Finally, Iceland is a destination that invites exploration at your own pace. Whether through guided tours or self-guided adventures, you'll find plenty of opportunities to find out hidden gems, from quiet hiking trails to remote fishing villages. The beauty of Iceland is not just in its well-known landmarks but also in the small moments—watching the sunset over a fjord, hearing the distant rumble of a waterfall, or standing in awe of the Northern Lights as they dance across the sky. These are the experiences that stay with you long after your trip is over, reminding you of the profound connection between nature and those who seek to look around it.

As you prepare to start on your trip to Iceland or reflect on your experiences there, remember that this country has something to offer every traveler. It's a place of adventure, tranquility, and culture. Whether you're returning home with photographs of the stunning landscapes, stories of your adventures, or a newfound appreciation for the power and beauty of nature, Iceland is sure to leave a lasting impression. Safe travels, and may your time in Iceland be as enriching as the country itself.

Made in the USA
Coppell, TX
07 February 2025

45550330R00174